Play Mathematics

by

HARRY LANGMAN, Ph. D.

Visiting Professor of Mathematics
Ball State Teachers College, Muncie, Indiana

HAFNER   PUBLISHING   COMPANY

New York · London

1962

PREFACE

Mathematical work is highly satisfying. So is mathematical play. And as most often is the case, one is apt to work much harder at any form of play, mental or physical, than one would for mere remuneration. Mathematical activity, more than any other, gives scope for the exercise of that faculty which has elevated man above other creatures.

However, most people, because of inadequate early instruction, are not equipped technically to indulge in such sport. Nevertheless there is great scope for play with mathematical ideas involving a minimum of technical knowledge and experience. This book is written largely for those with only such minimum knowledge. At the same time, it should be of interest to mathematical cognoscenti as well.

Most of the book may be read by any intelligent person with no mathematical knowledge beyond elementary arithmetic. It is recommended, however, that only the first part of Chapter X be read on a first perusal, unless one is specially interested in the procedure there discussed.

Explanations are given for a variety of types of problem. The exercises are all original, apart from the inevitable inclusion of some five or six simple ones that, presumably, are old. In these, as well as in the text, the author has relied entirely upon his own resources, without reference to any other work. In consequence, the choice of topics, and the relative attention given to each, reflect merely the degree of activity of the writer in those directions, and do not necessarily possess any greater significance. Many of these problems, in the form of puzzles, together with a great variety of puzzles of all kinds, quizzes and Minute Mysteries, have appeared in various magazines and newspapers, many under the pseudonym "Dr. Archimedes". A number of these were accompanied by special captions, brief stories and cartoons, most of which have been eliminated here.

References to the American Mathematical Monthly are designated by AMM, and to Scripta Mathematica by SM.

The author enjoys playing with such problems, particularly when he is able to find a solution of a technical problem by elementary means, and he believes others can learn to share such enjoyment. For those already initiated, this book offers new material and new ideas to play with. It is with both these objects in view that this book is offered.

December, 1950.   H. L.

CONTENTS

7

I   ARITHMETIC

Though a good part of the material in this book will consist of purely arithmetical developments, we shall in this chapter consider some matters that are specifically so, and follow with a list of graded exercises.

A number trick

We shall content ourselves with one example in this category. Before exhibiting this trick write down the numbers 715, 364, 924; as shown in the computation alongside. Then say to a friend, "Take a number, from 1 to 1000. Divide it by 7 and tell me the remainder." Suppose he announces that to be 4. You then ask, "What is the remainder on dividing your number by 11?" While that is being determined you multiply 715 by 4, getting 2860. Similarly, multiply 364 by the remainder on dividing by 11, and 924 by the remainder on dividing by 13. Adding these products, suppose we get 16664. Subtract the number of thousands, 16, from the rest of the number, 664, getting 648. This you announce as the number your friend took to start with. This will always work, except where the number of thousands is greater than the remainder of the number. For example, suppose the three remainders are, respectively, 1, 5, 7. The sum of the products is then 9003. In this case subtract 1 less than the number of thousands from what is then left, as shown in the computation to the left, to get the number, 995, yielding these remainders.

715	4	2860
364	10	3640
924	11	10164
		16664
		16
		648

9003
1003
8
995

That these figures will work is readily substantiated. Further, they may be derived arithmetically by an application of the method explained at the end of Chapter X.

An interesting problem

A number of six digits, on being multiplied by 6, yields a number of six digits which is identical with the first number, but having the first and second triads of digits interchanged. What is the number?

This, as we shall see, can be done in several ways (SM, March-June 1954, p. 145). From the proper viewpoint, as explained here, the problem can be solved without writing.

Suppose we visualize a third number, consisting of the sum of the two triad numbers of the first number. This number differs from the first number in that a number of thousands have been replaced by a number of ones, involving a reduction of as many 999's. That is, the third number differs from the first number by a multiple of 999. Similarly, the second number differs from the third number by replacing a certain number of ones by as many thousands; an increase of that many 999's. Hence the second number differs from the third number by some multiple of 999. Similarly the second number differs from the first number by a multiple of 999. But the second number is 6 times the first number. The difference between them is then 5 times the first number. Thus 5 times the first number is a multiple of 999. This requires that the first number itself must be a multiple of 999. So each of the other two numbers must be a multiple of 999. Now the third number is the sum of the two triad numbers. Obviously it cannot be as much as twice 999. Therefore it must be exactly 999. Now place the second number under the first number and add the two. Clearly, the sum of the two right-hand triads must be the third number, namely, 999. By the same token, the sum of the two left-hand triads must also be 999. Hence the sum of the two numbers must be 999999. But this sum must be 7 times the first number. The first number then, *if it exists*, must be one-seventh of 999999. This is 142857. Trying this out, we find it fits the conditions.

A problem in fractions

As we shall see in Chapter X, there are many types of problem which apparently require the use of algebra but which can be solved quite readily by the use of elementary arithmetic. Let us consider, for example, the following:

A common fraction has the value $\frac{1}{2}$. If 17 be added to the numerator, and 7 to the denominator, the value of the fraction is $\frac{2}{3}$. What is the fraction?

Let us write 17 above, and 7 below. We now visualize adding 1 successively to the upper number, and in each case 2 to the lower number till the proportion is 2 to 3. Now 1 has that proportion to $1\frac{1}{2}$. Hence the lower number has an excess of $\frac{1}{2}$ every time 1 is added to the upper and 2 to the lower number. But, to start with, the lower number is deficient of $25\frac{1}{2}$ (the number that is in the relation 3 to 2 with respect to the upper number) by $18\frac{1}{2}$. Every addition of 1 and 2 decreases this defect by $\frac{1}{2}$. Obviously, it requires 37 such additions to remove this defect. In other words, if 37 be added to the upper number and 74 to the lower we get the required proportion 2 to 3. Hence our fraction is $^{37}/_{74}$. (See Chapter X.)

The "Worst" question

Suppose we have a number of soldiers in a line. We ask, "What is the best alignment?" Let us suppose the men are equally thin, or thick, differing, essentially, only in height. Most people would say that the "best" array is one where increases (or decreases) in height go only in one direction. We shall not argue with that. We shall merely limit the last assertion to the requirement that the sum of the differences in height of adjacent men shall be a minimum. However, we now ask, "What is the 'worst' arrangement?" That is not so readily agreed upon. We might require, with some show of reason, that the sum of the differences in height of adjacent soldiers shall be a maximum. As we shall see presently, that is not at all determinate, since a number of different arrangements of the same group can share that maximum.

Suppose,* to begin with, that there are an odd number of men, say $2n+1$. Let their heights be a_k, where k goes from 1 to $2n+1$. Now let us arrange the men arbitrarily in a line. The sum of differences in height of adjacent pairs will have a definite value, say s. Now in this array suppose we find at least one triad in a row where the height of the middle one is between those of the other two. Clearly, s is not affected if we remove this soldier. Suppose we place him at either end. Obviously (unless the height of the end man is the same), we increase s by doing so, and the original array cannot be the "worst". Further, if in the new sequence the second is between the first and third in height, and we move the second to first position, we thereby increase s still further. Obviously, by following out this procedure, we reduce by 1 in each case the number of instances where a triad occurs with the middle height between the other two. Moreover, in each case, we increase s. Hence it follows that in the "worst" case the heights must zig-zag up and down as we go from one soldier to the next. Obviously, this zig-zag can take either of two forms:

I

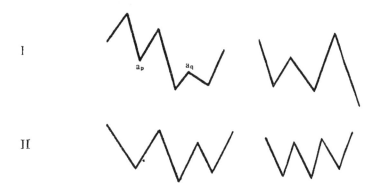

II

* For those unfamiliar with the use of letters to designate numbers, it is suggested that the outline only of the reasoning in this paragraph and the next be followed, particularly as applied to Exercise 43 at the end of this chapter

11

Now suppose that, in either type of array, some lower apex position, a_p, is greater than some upper apex position, a_q. It follows, then, that that sequence cannot be the "worst", since if we interchange the a_p and a_q heights, we increase s by $4(a_p-a_q)$. It follows, then, that in "the worst" sequence *no* upper apex is less than any lower apex.

Let us suppose that the $2n+1$ heights a_k conform to the sequence

$$a_1 \leqslant a_2 \leqslant a_3 \leqslant \cdots \leqslant a_{n+1} \leqslant \cdots \leqslant a_{2n} \leqslant a_{2n+1}. \tag{1}$$

From the last paragraph it follows then that, in Case I, the n upper values go from a_{n+2} to a_{2n+1}, and the $n+1$ lower values from a_1 to a_{n+1}; in Case II, the upper values go from a_{n+1} to a_{2n+1}, and the lower values from a_1 to a_n. If the extreme heights are x and y, we see at once that:

Case I, $\quad s = 2(a_{n+2}+a_{n+3}+\cdots+a_{2n+1})-[2(a_1+a_2+\cdots+a_{n+1})-(x+y)];$ (2a

Case II, $\quad s = [2(a_{n+1}+a_{n+2}+\cdots+a_{2n+1})-(x+y)]-2(a_1+a_2+\cdots+a_n).$ (2b

From the foregoing, s in (2a) is a maximum when $x+y$ is a maximum. Hence here

(I) $\qquad\qquad\qquad x+y=a_n+a_{n+1}.$ (3a

Also, in (2b), s is a maximum when $x+y$ is a minimum, or

(II) $\qquad\qquad\qquad x+y=a_{n+1}+a_{n+2}.$ (3b

Hence

(I) $\quad s = 2(a_{n+2}+a_{n+3}+\cdots+a_{2n+1})-[2(a_1+a_2+\cdots+a_{n+1})-(a_n+a_{n+1})];$ (4a

(II) $\quad s = [2(a_{n+1}+a_{n+2}+\cdots+a_{2n+1})-(a_{n+1}+a_{n+2})]-2(a_1+a_2+\cdots+a_n).$ (4b

We note then that, either in Case I or in Case II, we may permute the heights within the parentheses, other than the two taken for x and y, and get the same value of s. We have shown that s must be of this form and that it does not then matter how we permute the a's other than x and y. In other words, the "worst" arrangement has not as yet been defined so as to be unique.

Again, one of the two cases must give the maximum s. In general we cannot specify which.

Of course, we can now require that the peaks by themselves should have a "worst" sequence, and the same for the troughs. But the general statement appears troublesome.

Suppose now we have an even number of soldiers, $2n$. Here we have essentially one case, and it is readily seen that

$$s=[2(a_{n+1}+\cdots+a_{2n})-a_{n+1}]-[2(a_1+\cdots+a_n)-a_n]. \tag{4c}$$

These results will have to be modified somewhat if we consider the soldiers (or, in general, numbers) arrayed in a closed loop. We leave the formulation of them to the reader.

A cow problem

A certain breed of cow has the following characteristics: At the age of 3, and every year thereafter, it gives birth to a new female. Each of these goes through the same cycle. Now, disregarding males, and deaths, how many cows would there be in the herd after 20 years, if a farmer started with one such animal at birth?

This problem is typical of its kind. We shall view it here arithmetically, and shall then take it up again in the next chapter.

Years Hence	Number Born	Number 1 Year Old	Number 2 Years Old	Number Mature
0	1	0	0	0
1	0	1	0	0
2	0	0	1	0
3	1	0	0	1
4	1	1	0	1
5	1	1	1	1
6	2	1	1	2
7	3	2	1	3
8	4	3	2	4
9	6	4	3	6
10	9	6	4	9
11	13	9	6	13
12	19	13	9	19
13	28	19	13	28
14	41	28	19	41
15	60	41	28	60
16	88	60	41	88
17	129	88	60	129
18	189	129	88	189
19	277	189	129	277
20	406	277	189	406
21	595	406	277	595
22	872	595	406	872
23	1278	872	595	1278

In the table, in the first line, we have 1 new-born cow and no others. After 1 year we have no new-born cow, 1 one-year old cow and no others. Similarly after 2 years. However, after 3 years, we have 1 mature cow and also 1 new-born cow. Proceeding in this fashion, we complete our table. Let us examine it.

13

We note that every number in Column II occurs in Column III one line lower down, and in Column IV two lines lower. Further, excepting the first line, Columns II and V are identical. That is to be expected, since there must be one new-born for every mature cow.

Let us take a typical number in Column II, say 129 after 17 years. This occurs also in Column V in the same line. That number is the sum of the 88 above it, representing the number of mature cows the year before, and the 41 to the left, i.e. those that became mature in the interim. From what we have seen, the 88 occurs in Column II just before the 129, and the 41 also in Column II but two rows before the 88, namely, three rows before the 129. Clearly, this relationship is general, so that every number in Column II, from the fourth on, is the sum of the number immediately preceding it in the column and the one two rows before the latter. In other words, we do not need the other columns to obtain the figures in Column II, once we have the first three numbers, 1, 0, 0.

Again, let us view 129, typically, in Column V. As we have seen, it is the sum of the last two numbers in the line before: 41 and 88. Now 41 occurs in the line above in the previous column and 88 is the sum of the last two numbers in the second line above the 129. Hence 129 is the sum of the last three numbers two lines above. But each of the first two of these numbers occurs in the line above, one column to the left, and the third is the sum of the last two numbers in the line above it. Hence the 129 is the sum of the four numbers in the line three lines above it. That is true, then, of every number in the last column, hence of any number in the second column. Therefore the population of the herd after 20 years, i.e. the sum of the four numbers opposite 20 in column I, must also be the number in Column II opposite 23. The answer in this case is 1278.

We then see that we need only the numbers in Column II to determine the population for any year. We start with the column

$$1$$
$$0$$
$$0$$
$$\overline{}$$
$$1$$
$$\overline{}$$

and add figures below according to the law we have established. The nth number so added gives us the population of the herd after n years.

The last result should not be surprising, since, according to the terms of the problem, every cow alive will give birth to a new-born cow after three years, and no others in between. So the number of new-born cows three years hence will give the cow population now.

Nim games

To one who has analysed a "game" it is no longer a game but a certainty. Nevertheless such games offer some fascinating problems. Many forms can be described. One general form is as follows:

Two people play, each player alternately making a "move" which consists of removing at least 1 counter and at most m counters from one (and only one) of n piles of counters on a table. He loses (or, alternatively, wins) who is thus compelled (or able) to take the last counter from the table.

Here *m* may be taken as being indefinitely great. Given a distribution of counters in the *n* piles, can either player so determine his play that he is sure to win? This question is readily answered for the problem as stated. Such a solution can presumably be found elsewhere. However, we shall formulate the solution for the special case where m=3 and n=3. In this case the player whose turn it is to move notes the remainders he obtains on dividing the numbers in each pile by 4. He then notes that if these do not form one of the five sets shown below he can be certain of winning. If they do, his opponent can be certain of winning.

$$0, \ 0, \ 1;$$
$$0, \ 2, \ 2;$$
$$0, \ 3, \ 3;$$
$$1, \ 1, \ 1;$$
$$1, \ 2, \ 3.$$

The point is that a player cannot get one such set by playing from any one of them, but he can get one such set (generally in three ways) from any other set of remainders. That means that once a player is caught in such a predicament he cannot get out. In that event, if his opponent has not analysed the play, the player can merely take one counter at random and hope that the other player makes a "slip".

Another form of NIM is to have a single pile of counters, a player winning or losing, if he, or his opponent, ends with an odd, or an even number of counters. The writer has analysed this for one and for two piles. The general solution seems troublesome.

Prime numbers

We note that a prime number is an integer not divisible by any smaller integer other than 1. Many fascinating problems require integers for solutions. Among these are many restricted to primes. For reference later, we give the following list:

Prime numbers less than 1000

1	101	211	307	401	503	601	701	809	907
2	103	223	311	409	509	607	709	811	911
3	107	227	313	419	521	613	719	821	919
5	109	229	317	421	523	617	727	823	929
7	113	233	331	431	541	619	733	827	937
11	127	239	337	433	547	631	739	829	941
13	131	241	347	439	557	641	743	839	947
17	137	251	349	443	563	643	751	853	953
19	139	257	353	449	569	647	757	857	967
23	149	263	359	457	571	653	761	859	971
29	151	269	367	461	577	659	769	863	977
31	157	271	373	463	587	661	773	877	983
37	163	277	379	467	593	673	787	881	991
41	167	281	383	479	599	677	797	883	997
43	173	283	389	487		683		887	
47	179	293	397	491		691			
53	181			499					
59	191								
61	193								
67	197								
71	199								
73									
79									
83									
89									
97									

Comments on Exercises

12, 13, 14. Any year in recent centuries may be arrived at in this way, generally in several ways.

15. Imagine that the library contained just one extra book.

49, 50. First factor the given numbers into primes.

53, 54, 55, 56. Suppose we wish to find the smallest integer written with 1's or 1's and one or more 0's which is divisible by 119. Remembering that 119 is 7×17, we form the following table:

0	1	2	3	4	5	6	7	8	9	10	11	12	13	14	15	16	17
1	10	15	14	4	6	9	5	16	7	2	3	13	11	8	2	1	10
1	3	2	6	4	5	1	3	2	6	4	5	1	3	2	6	4	5

We note that the number required is the sum of several numbers each consisting of 1 with a number of 0's. In the table we show in the second line what the remainder is if we divide 1 with as many 0's after it as is shown in the first row by 17. In the third row we do the same with 7 as a divisor. We seek to find the group of numbers furthest to the left where the sum of the remainders in the second line is 17, 34, 51, etc. Of these we pick the smallest where the sum of the remainders in the last line is 7, 14, 21, 28, 35, or a larger multiple of 7.

34. Cf. Ex. 18, Ch. II, Ex. 38, Ch. IV.

65. "The Million Puzzle". This is an example of one of a number of types the writer has prepared for a special purpose. It is rather difficult to see how mathematical technique can be applied to such a problem. This type can, in fact, be made very difficult.

Exercises

1. July 4, 1776 fell on what day of the week?

2. What day of the week was it exactly one century ago?

Four problems in mental arithmetic:

3. 16 is one and one-third times what number?

4. 15 is one and one-quarter times more than what number?

5. Four-digit numbers are formed with 1, 2, 3, 4 in all possible ways, each number containing all the four digits. What is the sum of all these numbers?

6. Four-digit numbers are formed in all possible ways with each number containing the digits 4, 5, 7, 9. What is the sum of all of these numbers?

7. A cashier was asked to give 14 coins as correct change for a dollar. In how many different ways could he do so?

8. In Ex. 7, suppose he gave 15 coins as change. ·

9. In Ex. 7, suppose he gave 16 coins as change.

10. In Ex. 7, suppose he gave 17 coins as change.

11. In Ex. 7, suppose he gave 18 coins as change.

12.

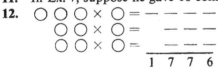

Distribute the digits from 1 to 0, one in each circle, so that the sum of the products indicated will be 1776 (SM. June, 1948, p. 163).

13. In Ex. 12, replace 1776 by 1492.

14. In Ex. 12, replace 1776 by the current year.

15. A librarian spent a holiday arranging the books on the shelves. He tried to arrange them in groups of 7, but the last group was one short. The

17

last group was also one short when he tried groups of 8, 9, 10, 11, after which he gave up. Knowing that the number of books was under 50000, determine how many there actually were.

16. — — —   This represents an ordinary addition where all the digits
— — —   from 1 to 9 were used. Reconstruct it.
— — —

17. CROSS-FIGURES. A single digit goes in each space, forming four four-digit numbers in each direction.

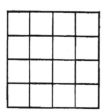

ROWS: 1) This is a prime number (not divisible by any other number except itself and 1). It is less than 2000, is 2 more than a perfect square and the sum of its digits is 11.

2) Apart from 1, all its factors are even.

3) The number represented by the first two digits is 2 more than that represented by the last two. The number represented by the first and third digits is four times that represented by the second and fourth digits. The sum of all the digits is 23.

4) This is a multiple of 3, 137, and another prime number. The sum of its digits is over 24.

COLUMNS: 1) This is an even multiple of 11; also of 29.

2) This is a multiple of 239. The first two digits represent a multiple of 25. .

3) The digits are in increasing arithmetical progression and have the sum 20.

4) This is less than 4000 and does not contain a 2. It is divisible by 9, with a quotient that is a prime number with the last two digits equal.

18. CROSS-FIGURES.

A	B
3 9 0 5	6 3 1
1 3 0 7	4 2 7

ACROSS: 1) The difference of the A numbers, less 1000.

5) Average of the B numbers.

18

8) Average of the A numbers.

9) The smaller of the A numbers, less the larger of the B numbers.

10) This is a multiple of 29, and the first digit is the sum of the other two.

11) Sum of the larger of A and the smaller of B.

12) This is an odd square number with the first digit greater than the last. It differs by a square number from the number of days in an ordinary year.

14) This is less than 44. It is an odd multiple of 3 and 5.

15) This is the largest prime number less than 100.

17) This is the number of cubic inches in a gallon.

19) A square number divisible by both 5 and 17.

21) This is one-tenth the average of the A numbers, to the nearest unit.

24) This is an odd multiple of 3. The sum of the digits is less than 12. The first digit is 4 more than the last, which is 1 more than the middle digit.

25) The sum of the A numbers plus twice the sum of the B numbers.

26) A multiple of 11. The sum of the first two digits is 4, that of the last two 10.

27) This is half the remainder after subtracting 1183 from the difference between the product of the larger of A with the smaller of B and that of the smaller of A and twice the larger of B.

DOWN: 1) The next prime number after 113.

2) The average of the B numbers plus the sum of the digits of both the sum and the difference of the A numbers, less 1.

3) The digits of this are the same as those of the larger of A. This is not divisible by 5, but is divisible by 11, giving a quotient not containing a 4.

4) This is twice a prime number. It differs by 18 from its reversal, which is 4 times a prime number.

5) This is a prime number where the middle digit is twice the third, and the first digit is 1 less than that.

6) 125 plus the average of A.

7) This is a multiple of 11, with the sum of its digits 22. The second digit is 1 more than the fourth, and the first 1 less than twice the fourth.

11) 100 more than a prime number with the second digit less than the third, and the first, a square number, equal to the sum of the other two.

13) A square number. The first digit is three times the second and 1 more than the third.

15) The digits are in descending arithmetical progression and total 24.

16) 324 plus 13 times the average of the B numbers.

18) This is twice an odd number. The digits are in arithmetical progression.

20) This is divisible by 3. The first digit is greater than the second and the third is three times the sum of the other two.

22) An even multiple of 31. The digits decrease from left to right. The middle digit is even.

19

23) This is the difference of the squares of two numbers which differ by 7. The units digit is the sum of the other two.

25) This is 5 times the B sum, diminished by the A sum.

19.

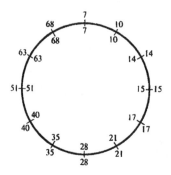

a) Arrange the numbers inside the circle so that every adjacent pair shall have a common factor other than 1.

b) Arrange the numbers outside the circle so that every adjacent pair shall be relatively prime (have no common factor other than 1).

20. $— — \times — — + — — — + — — — = 1949.$

Arrange the ten digits from 0 to 9, one for each dash, so that the given sum will be obtained.

21. $2 \times 7 + 4 \times 6 + 5 \times 9 + 18 + 3 = 100.$

This is incorrect, but will be correct if two digits be interchanged.

22. Divide this area into four sections by two straight lines so that the sum of the numbers in each shall be the same.

XI	IV	X	V
	VIII		VI
		III	
XII	VII I	IX	II

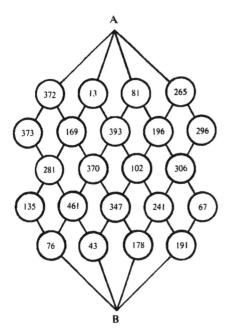

23. There are 50 ways of going from A to B through five circles. In one way the sum of the numbers in the five circles passed through is 1000. How quickly can you find that way?

24. Moving cyclically, transfer two numbers from each column to the next on the right (and from the last to the first) so that all columns will have the same sum.

167	131	210	112	178	148
98	111	204	197	114	113
203	217	85	188	165	99
185	186	222	129	196	224
117	156	95	120	179	168
135	233	166	340	144	265
905	1034	982	1086	976	1017

25. A boy was telling his father that his teacher had prepared three baskets of marbles labelled A, B, and C, and had then asked six pupils in turn to do the following:

a) Put one-third of the marbles in A into B;
b) put one-fifth of the marbles now in B into C;
c) put one-half of the marbles now in C into A;
d) put one-half of the marbles now in A into B;
e) put one-third of the marbles now in B into C;
f) put one-fifth of the marbles now in C into A.

At this point all the baskets contained the same number of marbles. When asked how many marbles the baskets had contained originally, the boy had forgotten, except that the marbles in B and C together totalled over 500 but less than 540. Being a clever man, the boy's father deduced how many marbles each basket contained. Can you also determine this?

26. If 1 be added to the numerator of a fraction, and 1 subtracted from the denominator, the fraction reduces to $\frac{2}{3}$. If instead we add 4 to the numerator, and 7 to the denominator, the fraction reduces to $\frac{5}{8}$. What is the fraction? (See also Chapters II and X.)

27. A fraction has the value $\frac{1}{2}$. If 17 be added to the numerator, and 7 to the denominator, the fraction reduces to $\frac{2}{3}$. What is the fraction? (See also Chapters II and X.)

28. A fraction has the value $\frac{2}{3}$. If 332 be deducted from the numerator, and 244 from the denominator, the new fraction has the value $\frac{1}{2}$. Find the fraction.

29. A fraction has the value $\frac{2}{3}$. If 62 be added to the numerator, and 592 to the denominator, the fraction reduces to $\frac{4}{7}$. Find the fraction.

30. A common fraction has the value $\frac{1}{2}$. If 1347 be added to the numerator and 882 to the denominator the new fraction has the value $\frac{2}{3}$. Find the fraction.

31. If we add 16 to the numerator of a fraction and subtract 166 from the denominator, the fraction reduces to $\frac{3}{4}$. If instead we add 124 to the numerator and 340 to the denominator, the fraction reduces to $\frac{1}{2}$. Find the fraction.

32. If 170 be subtracted from the numerator of a fraction and 2137 added to the denominator, the fraction reduces to $\frac{2}{5}$. If instead 141 be added to the numerator and 160 subtracted from the denominator, the fraction reduces to $\frac{4}{5}$. Find the fraction.

33. If the numerator of a fraction be reduced by 1113 and the denominator by 2114, the new fraction has the value $\frac{7}{8}$. If instead the numerator be reduced by 178, and the denominator increased by 4893, the new fraction has the value $\frac{3}{7}$. What is the fraction?

34. (Cf. Ex. 18, Ch. II and Ex. 38, Ch. IV.) What is the smallest integer with units digit 7 in which the transfer of this 7 to the leading position is equivalent to subtracting 1 and then multiplying by 2?

35.

0 ZERO	6 SIX
1 ONE	7 SEVEN
2 TWO	8 EIGHT
3 THREE	9 NINE
4 FOUR	10 TEN
5 FIVE	

Associate with each of the eleven numbers given above the sum obtained by adding up the numbers representing the sequential positions in the alphabet of the letters alongside. Then divide these numbers into two groups so that the totals of the numbers shall be in the same proportion as the totals of their associated numbers.

36. A commuter bought presents for his nephews, the bill coming to a whole number of dollars, but not a whole number of tens. On the train he amused himself by writing out the amount in the form of "So many hundred and so many dollars." To his surprise, he found that, if in that expression he replaced each letter by its numbered position in the alphabet, the total of these was the amount of the bill. What was the total?

37. A parchment dating from the time of Charlemagne was on a table before a mirror. The top of the parchment dropped over the back of the table before the mirror. The date, in Roman numerals, on that portion of the parchment, was readable correctly even as reflected by the mirror. In Arabic notation, this date was represented by a prime number with three different digits. What was the date?

38. A printer cast special numerals for the page numbers of a de luxe edition of a certain work of 1762 pages. How many of each digit did he cast?

38A. Arrange the numbers from 1 to 15 in groups of three, each in arithmetical progression and with the five common differences all different. There are two solutions (See SM, Sept. 1950, p. 215).

39.

21	45	Separate these ten numbers into two groups of
22	65	five numbers each so that the product of the numbers
34	76	in each group shall be the same.
39	133	
44	153	

40.

433	932	Arrange these eight three-digit numbers in four pairs
569	367	so that the sum of the products of each pair shall
201	125	be a six-digit number consisting of an arrangement
553	486	of the digits 1, 2, 4, 5, 6, 7.

41. A fraction has the value $^7/_9$. If we add 1154 to the numerator and a certain integer between 1168 and 1202 to the denominator the fraction then has the value $^{19}/_{22}$. What is the fraction? (See also Chapters II and X.)

42. Arrange the numbers from 1 to 51 in 17 triads so that the sum of the numbers in each triad shall be the same. (See Chapter VI.)

43. Dates for Mental Digestion: There are two coins, a dime and an older coin, a cent, both of this century. The date on the older coin is a prime of four different digits. The sum of the two dates is a prime number. So is the difference. If the sum and difference be added we get a number which has only two distinct prime factors, one of which occurs to the fifth power. What are the dates? (Note: A fifth power is the result of using a number five times as a factor. For example, the fifth power of 7 is $7 \times 7 \times 7 \times 7 \times 7$, or 16807.)

44. One three-digit number is three times another three-digit number. If we reverse the digits in each number the second is four times the first. What are the numbers?

45. A certain four-digit number may be represented just as accurately by the use of three of these four digits without any other mark. Five numbers possess this characteristic. What are they? (Note: The fifth power of 7 is represented in the notation 7^5.)

46. Adding 1 to the first of two numbers gives one-third more than the second. Adding 1 to the second gives one-fifth less than the first. What are the numbers? (See Ch. X.)

47. Two fractions total 1. Transferring 4 from the numerator of the smaller to that of the larger makes the latter three times the former. Adding 10 to both the numerator and the denominator of the smaller reduces that fraction to one-half. What are the fractions? (See Ch. X.)

48. Twelve soldiers have heights 5′ 4½″, 5′ 5½″, 5′ 6″, 5′ 6½″, 5′ 7½″, 5′ 8″, 5′ 8½″, 5′ 9½″, 5′ 10″, 5′ 11½″, 6′ 0″, 6′ 1″. They are arrayed so that the sum of the differences in height of adjacent pairs is a maximum. What is that maximum value?

49. — — — — — $\times$ — — — — — $= 1\,0\,3\,4\,7\,0\,5\,0\,0\,0$. This represents the product of two five-digit numbers which together comprise all the ten different digits. What are the numbers?

50. In Ex. 49, suppose the product is $2\,2\,3\,8\,2\,0\,0\,0\,0\,0$. What are the factors?

51. A number under 50000 has the remainder 7 on dividing by 29; the remainder 11 on dividing by 30; the remainder 13 on dividing by 31. What is the number? (Cf. Ch. X.)

52. There are less than 50 digits in a certain number. The leading digits are 67. Now if we add 67, then divide by 6, and then move the last two digits to the extreme left, we come back to the original number. What is it? (Cf. Ex. 26, Ch. II, also Comments on Ex. 18, Ch. II.)

53. What is the smallest number divisible by 21 which in ordinary notation is written only with 1's, or 1's and one or more 0's?

54. What is the smallest such number that is divisible by 259?

55. What is the smallest such number that is divisible by 4403?

56. What is the smallest such number that is divisible by 2295?

57. PEMBERTON CAMP   NEWTON STATION

Albemarle and Pemberton were two rival schools for boys, each of which maintained a summer camp. One afternoon a baseball game was arranged

at the Pemberton Camp. The Albemarle team, with its contingent of rooters, took the train to Newton and then filled three buses which had been chartered to take them all to the Pemberton Camp. They were warned that the last train back to Albemarle left at 7 p.m.

During the game a multiple car crash was reported and two of the three buses were commandeered to carry men and supplies to the scene. When by 4.30 the buses had not returned some of the Albemarle boys began to worry.

But Pluto Smith, a promising young mathematician, thought there might be a solution to the dilemma. "How far is it to Newton," he asked the driver. "Twenty-one miles," was the answer. "How fast can you go safely?" "Thirty-six miles an hour," said the driver; "there isn't enough time to make the trip three times."

Pluto scratched some markings in the sandy ground. "We are trained to walk steadily at four miles an hour," he said. "It seems to me that if the game is finished by 5 p.m. we can make it to Newton with several minutes to spare." The driver was sceptical, but was soon convinced. The ball game was over just before five and all the Albemarle boys caught the seven o'clock train at Newton.

Can you explain how this was managed?

58. Break up the ten digits so as to make five prime numbers, subject to the condition that each is less than 1000, the largest has no number 7, one prime is half the sum of two others, and the sum of all the primes is 45 times a prime number.

59.　　　　　—　　This represents a distribution of the ten digits so
　　　　　　— —　　that four prime numbers are formed having the
　　　　　— — —　　required sum. The third number is over 8 times
　　　　— — — —　　the second. What are the numbers?

　　　 4　8　0　6

60. Three prime numbers, each greater than 22, have the sum 131. One is 1 more than twice another. The six digits used in writing these primes are all different. What are the numbers?

61. Another number trick.

Ask someone to take a number under 1000, divide it by 27 and give the remainder; then by 37 and give the remainder. Suppose these remainders are 19 and 36 respectively. Show that by using the "magic" numbers 703 and 297, as in the following computation, the required number will be obtained:

$$19 \times 703 = 13357$$
$$36 \times 297 = \underline{10692}$$
$$24049$$
$$\underline{24}$$
$$73$$

In the last, the number of thousands is added to what is left of the number to get the required number (if this gives 1000 or more add the 1 to the rest of the number).

62. Antedating Coins. A wealthy numismatist said to his talented nephew on the latter's birthday: "I have selected five valuable coins which I shall present to you if you can determine the dates on all of them from what I now tell you. The oldest coin is dated 1100 and the most recent before 1300. The sum of all the five dates contains no digit 7. When I arrange the coins in line according to date, the difference between the dates of every adjacent pair is a prime number. Further, the difference in the dates between every pair separated by one coin is twice a prime number. Also, the difference of each pair separated by two coins is three times a prime number. And finally, the difference between the first and last is four times a prime number. Moreover, all the ten prime numbers referred to are different. What are the dates?" History says the promising young man worked all night, and found the answers. How about you?

63. A Prime Difficulty. This represents an arrangement of the digits from 1 to 9 with the following properties:

— — — a) One horizontal three-digit number is the mean between
— — — the other two.
— — — b) Two horizontal numbers are prime.

c) The sum of the digits of the largest is also a prime number.

d) Two of the three-digit numbers formed, reading downwards, are also prime.

Can you reconstruct the arrangement?

64. Another Prime Teaser. Here also we have an arrangement of the digits from 1 to 9. Two of the horizontal three-digit numbers
— — — are prime. The third is the mean of the other two but is
— — — itself 3 times a prime. The smallest number is at the top,
— — — the largest at the bottom. Two such arrangements are possible. Can you find them?

65. The Million Puzzle.

110471	92362	297850	63092	173209
21339	147691	148325	149713	60453
214683	10391	23597	18139	110578
5909	216535	88248	43658	4942
38204	6577	9678	13968	256789
286341	41639	13542	111547	124207
61485	307284	149735	31217	26390
96873	50021	210429	30274	34146
152097	24054	9993	244306	46821
12598	103446	48603	294086	162465
1000000	1000000	1000000	1000000	1000000

52358	112653	7163	113923	28353
279333	161417	109763	80296	14064
154624	249305	33247	7051	320024
29432	28894	210491	30277	161632
33641	7252	118002	42436	40828
105792	58248	21945	302761	18467
101630	127910	70574	104789	72143
203521	18039	145328	38618	200693
23607	32562	263357	60545	22091
16062	203720	20130	219304	121705
1000000	1000000	1000000	1000000	1000000

Here we have ten sets of ten numbers each, with each set totalling 1000000. The problem is to select one number from each of the ten sets so that the sum of the ten numbers thus selected shall be 1000000, or as close as possible thereto.

66. A Clever lad, applying for a job as assistant bookkeeper, had a long wait in the anteroom. Through a partition he then overheard the following conversation between his prospective employers:

A. "The contractor on Dean Street has ordered some of our new small size blue tiles, the $\frac{5}{8}''$ cubes. He wants from 16 to 18 thousand of them.

B. "Suppose we use one of our new packing cases. The waste spaces can be filled as usual with cardboard. Their inner dimensions are in whole numbers of inches, aren't they?

A. "Yes, just as we ordered. This one is about right. It holds exactly 16524 tiles at the most. Funny! If it were twice as high it would hold 34020 tiles of this size.

B. "H'm, yes! And if it were three times as long it would hold 50490 tiles.

A. "The queer part of it is that if it were four times as wide it would hold only 66096 tiles.

B. "Right you are! So it figures. 'Tis funny".

Not finding it necessary to count on his fingers, the boy was able to amuse himself by deducing from the foregoing the inner dimensions of the carton discussed. (Incidentally, he got the job!) Can you duplicate the feat of the bright young fellow?

67. In the cow problem (page 13), suppose each cow died at approximately $7\frac{1}{2}$ years of age. What would the population then be after 20 years?

27

II ALGEBRA

To the mathematician all mathematics is good fun, and there is but a minor distinction between mathematical work and mathematical play. To one with but a smattering of mathematical knowledge, however, there is a wider distinction in the fact that mathematical recreation, though smacking essentially of mathematics, requires a minimum of mathematical knowledge and technique. Thus where the skilled mathematician can nonchalantly exhibit his virtuosity in elegant manipulation and the ready solution of apparently difficult problems, the unskilled finds such a performance completely beyond his scope. Thus there are many thousands of problems which permit of tricky and gratifying solutions by skilled algebraic manipulation, but they could hardly come within the scope of this book, where a minimum of technical knowledge is presupposed.

So the writer will offer very little under algebraic recreation as such; leaving illustrations and occasional brief discussions of algebraic treatment to the exercises that follow and to its application in the following chapters.

A number trick

The following is self-explanatory.

What you say to the audience	*What you visualize*
Write down any number.	x
Multiply this number by 6.	$6x$
Subtract 1.	$6x - 1$
Multiply this number by itself.	$36x^2 - 12x + 1$
Add 23 to that.	$36x^2 - 12x + 24$
Divide this by 24.	$(3x^2 - x)/2 + 1$
Subtract 1.	$(3x^2 - x)/2$
Multiply by 2.	$3x^2 - x$
Now divide this product by the number you first wrote down (oh, yes, it will come out even!).	$3x - 1$
Add 40 to the quotient.	$3x + 39$
Divide this by 3.	$x + 13$
From this quotient subtract the number you first wrote down.	13

Your answer is 13!

This procedure can be varied ad lib.

The cow problem

We again consider the problem discussed in Chapter I and give it an algebraic formulation.

Let a_n be the cow population after n years from the birth of the first cow. Then $a_0 = a_1 = a_2 = 1$. From what we learned before, we may write

$$a_{n+3} = a_{n+2} + a_n, \quad n = 1, 2, 3, \cdots. \tag{1}$$

Let

$$y = a_0 + a_1 x + a_2 x^2 + a_3 x^3 + \cdots. \tag{2}$$

Then

$$xy = a_0 x + a_1 x^2 + a_2 x^3 + \cdots,$$
$$x^3 y = \qquad\qquad a_0 x^3 + \cdots.$$

We have then, in the light of (1),

$$(1 - x - x^3)y = a_0 + (a_1 - a_0)x + (a_2 - a_1)x^2$$
$$= 1.$$

Hence

$$y = \frac{1}{1 - x - x^3} = \frac{1}{1 - (x + x^3)}$$
$$= x(1 + x^2) + x^2(1 + x^2)^2 + x^3(1 + x^2)^3 + \cdots. \tag{3}$$

In (2), a_n is the coefficient of x^n. Hence a_n is the coefficient of x^n in (3) also. Hence the cow population after 20 years is the coefficient of x^{20} in (3). That is clearly the coefficient of x^{20} in

$$x^8(1 + x^2)^8 + x^{10}(1 + x^2)^{10} + x^{12}(1 + x^2)^{12} + x^{14}(1 + x^2)^{14} + x^{16}(1 + x^2)^{16}$$
$$+ x^{18}(1 + x^2)^{18} + x^{20}(1 + x^2)^{20}.$$

That is,

$$\frac{8 \cdot 7}{1 \cdot 2} + \frac{10 \cdot 9 \cdot 8 \cdot 7 \cdot 6}{1 \cdot 2 \cdot 3 \cdot 4 \cdot 5} + \frac{12 \cdot 11 \cdot 10 \cdot 9}{1 \cdot 2 \cdot 3 \cdot 4} + \frac{14 \cdot 13 \cdot 12}{1 \cdot 2 \cdot 3} + \frac{16 \cdot 15}{1 \cdot 2} + 18 + 1$$
$$= 28 + 252 + 495 + 364 + 120 + 18 + 1 = 1278,$$

as before.

Comments on Exercises

15. If the triads are A and B, the first number is $1000A + B$.

18. Suppose n digits precede the 7 in units place. Then the number may be written $10A + 7$, where A contains n digits. From the statement of the problem,

$$2(10A + 6) = 7 \cdot 10^n + A, \text{ or } 19A = 7 \cdot 10^n - 12.$$

Now divide $7000 \cdots$ by 19 until the remainder 12 is first obtained. (Cf. Exs. 33 and 36, also Ch. I.)

19. Let a permissible time be such that the hour hand is x minute spaces after a hours past XII, and the minute hand y minute spaces past b hours after XII. Here a and b are integers and each less than 12, and x and y each less than 5.

Then

$$\frac{5b + y}{12} = x.$$

Also, if the hands are reversible,

$$\frac{5a + x}{12} = y.$$

From these two equations we have,

$$x = \frac{5a + 60b}{143}, \qquad y = \frac{5b + 60a}{143}.$$

Now see for what values of a and b consistent values for x and y are obtained.

26. Let n digits follow the figures 67. Then the number may be represented by $67 \cdot 10^n + A$. Now, according to the conditions of the problem, we may write

$$\frac{67(10^n + 1) + A}{6} = 100A + 67,$$

whence

$$67(10^n - 5) = 599A.$$

Now divide 9999 ⋯ ⋯ ⋯ by 599 until the remainder 4 is obtained (corresponding to an exact division of 999999 ⋯ ⋯ ⋯ 5 by 599), multiply by 67 to get A, then prefix the 67.

33. What solutions are possible?

40. The remarks here apply with but slight modification to Exercises 38, 39, 41, 42.

Suppose that the two factor numbers, on being divided by 9, yield remainders a and b, each less than 9. Since the digits are the same on the right, the remainder must be $a + b$ or, if this is 9 or more, 9 less than that. At any rate the product of the two numbers a and b differs from their sum by some multiple of 9. This is indicated by the symbolism

$$a \cdot b \equiv a + b \quad (9).$$

This may be written

$$ab - a - b \equiv 0 \quad (9),$$

which means that the quantity on the left is a multiple of 9. We have then

$$(a - 1)(b - 1) \equiv 1 \quad (9).$$

This means that the two factors must be so chosen that their product is 1 more than a multiple of 9. Permissible combinations are:

$$a - 1:\ 1, 2, 5, 4, 7, 8;$$
$$b - 1:\ 1, 5, 2, 7, 4, 8.$$

In other words, a and b must have remainders 2 and 2, 3 and 6, 5 and 8, 0 and 0 (the last meaning that each factor is a multiple of 9). This restricts the possibilities of choice enough to make the detailed examination practicable.

42. Here a two-digit number times a three-digit number gives a five-digit number and all three of the numbers comprise the ten digits. Here we have the tedious job of finding all such products. To facilitate this, let the remainders of the three numbers on dividing by 9 be a, b, c. Here $a + b + c = 0$ or a multiple of 9. Hence $a + b + ab$ must be a (possibly zero) multiple of 9. Hence $(a + 1)(b + 1)$ must be 1 more than a (possibly zero) multiple of 9. The numbers $a + 1$ and $b + 1$ must then have the values 1 and 1, 2 and 5, 4 and 7, or 8 and 8. We have thus the six cases:

	a	b
I	0	0
II	1	4
III	3	6
IV	4	1
V	6	3
VI	7	7

Under Case I, for example, we write in a column the permissible numbers for a: 27, 36, 45, 54, 63, 72. Opposite each of these we write all the permissible numbers for b. For example, opposite 27 we have: 396, 459, 468, 486, 504, 513, 549, 594, 603, 639, 648, 684, 693, 819, 846, 864, 918, 936, 954, 963. Having done this for all admissible numbers, the multiplications are carried out. Of course, most of the pairings are rejected at a glance. In this way a total of nine solutions is obtained. It will be noted that in these each of two five-digit numbers is obtained in more than one way. Referring to the dialog, the set of three numbers sought is obtained uniquely.

Exercises

1. Solve Ex. 26 of Ch. I algebraically.
2. Solve Ex. 27 of Ch. I algebraically.
3. Solve Ex. 28 of Ch. I algebraically.
4. Solve Ex. 29 of Ch. I algebraically.
5. Solve Ex. 30 of Ch. I algebraically.
6. Solve Ex. 31 of Ch. I algebraically.
7. Solve Ex. 32 of Ch. I algebraically.
8. Solve Ex. 33 of Ch. I algebraically.
9. Solve Ex. 34 of Ch. I algebraically.
10. Solve Ex. 46 of Ch. I algebraically.

11. Solve Ex. 47 of Ch. I algebraically.

12. Solve Ex. 11 of Ch. X algebraically.

13. Solve Ex. 12 of Ch. X algebraically.

14. Solve Ex. 13 of Ch. X algebraically.

15. A six-digit number has its two triads interchanged on being multiplied by 6. What is the number? (See Ch. I.)

16. Solve Ex. 14 of Ch. X algebraically.

17. Solve Ex. 15 of Ch. X algebraically.

18. (See Ex. 38 of Ch. IV.) What is the smallest number with units digit 7 in which transferring this 7 to the leading position is equivalent to subtracting 1 and then multiplying by 2?

19. How many times in 12 hours may the hands of a clock be interchanged and still indicate a possibly correct time?

20. Show that if each of two two-digit numbers AB and BC is divisible by 7 (or 13), then CA is also divisible by 7 (or 13).

21. (See Ex. 17, Ch. IV.) What five-digit number is reversed on multiplying by 4?

22. What five-digit number is reversed on being multiplied by 9?

23. In Exs. 21 and 22, will any other multiplier serve?

24. Twice A's age plus three times B's age total 133 years. 5 years hence B will be twice as old as A was when A was 4 years older than half of what B was the year before. How old is each?

25. Solve Ex. 41, Ch. I algebraically.

26. Solve Ex. 52, Ch. I algebraically.

27. Using the digits from 1 to 9 once each, form three three-digit numbers in which they are in arithmetical progression, the extremes are primes, and the middle number is three times a prime. Find all solutions.

28. Simms and Watkins, salesmen of washing machines and radios, compared notes. Each item was standard and sold for a whole number of dollars. Curiously, though Simms had sold 10 washing machines and 17 radios, and Watkins had sold 7 washing machines and 30 radios, their total sales for the week were the same, and their commissions, at 4%, though under $80 each, better than Hodsdon's $72.50. What did each item sell for?

29. Elusive Billiard Balls. All the balls, numbered from 1 to 15, have been pocketed. We have the following information:

1) The total of the numbers in F equals the total of the numbers in B plus the number of balls in E.

2) The sum of the numbers in A and E is 1 more than those in B and D.

3) A has no even-numbered ball.

4) The number on one ball in F is twice that of another.

5) The total of the numbers in C equals the number of balls in it.

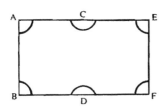

6) The 13 ball is not in A, E or F.

7) The totals in A and B are the same.

8) B and E have the same number of balls.

9) D has two balls more than A.

10) F has 1 ball less than D.

11) B has no number 5, does not consist of even numbers only and has no odd number greater than 9.

12) A's total is 2 more than D's.

Can you deduce how the balls were distributed?

30. Solve Ex. 41 of Ch. I algebraically.

31. Solve Ex. 34 algebraically.

32. Reversion of Sales. An employee of a New York bicycle concern, on his way back after a short vacation, overheard three salesmen of a rival concern in another city discussing their earnings on the last full business day before the holiday. He noted down whatever information he could gather and reported this knowledge to his chief, substantially as follows:

The salesmen, whom he could identify only as A, B and C, sold only three different items, tricycles, bicycles and motorcycles, at fixed prices; each a whole number of dollars exclusive of tax. All told, 9 tricycles, 15 bicycles and 16 motorcycles were sold. A's sales totalled $ 1210, B's $ 1794, C's $ 1743. Commissions at 6% for tricycles, 4% for bicycles and 3% for motorcycles netted A $ 42.96, B $ 57.87 and C $ 60.39. From this information the sales manager was able to compute the sale price of each of the items. Can you? And can you determine also how many of each article each salesman sold?

33. (See Ex. 49, Ch. IV.) Moving the units digit of a certain number to the leading position is equivalent to multiplying the number by 7. How many digits has the number?

34. Jane's age and John's age together now total 70 years. Twelve years hence John will be five times as old as Jane was at the time when both together were 10 years older than Jane will be when both together will be ten times as old as Jane was when John was 3 years younger than he is now. How old is Jane?

35. Solve Ex. 23 of Ch. X algebraically.

36. Solve Ex. 24 of Ch. X algebraically.

37. Solve Ex. 25 of Ch. X algebraically.

38. $\dfrac{-\ -\ -\ -\ -}{-\ -\ -\ -\ -} = \dfrac{4\ 3}{1\ 1\ 1}$

The fraction on the left comprises all the ten digits. Find all solutions.

39. $\dfrac{-\ -}{-\ -} = \dfrac{-\ -\ -}{-\ -\ -}$

The digits used in writing these fractions comprise all ten. Find all solutions.

40. $\bigcirc\bigcirc \times \bigcirc\bigcirc = \bigcirc\bigcirc\bigcirc\bigcirc$

The product of two two-digit numbers is a four-digit number composed of the same four digits as in the factor numbers. Find all solutions.

41. $\bigcirc\bigcirc\bigcirc \times \bigcirc = \bigcirc\bigcirc\bigcirc\bigcirc$

The product of a three-digit number by a number of one digit is a four-digit number composed of the same four digits as the factor numbers. Find all solutions.

42. (See the last two problems.)

$\bigcirc\bigcirc \times \bigcirc\bigcirc = \bigcirc\bigcirc\bigcirc\bigcirc$
$\bigcirc\bigcirc\bigcirc \times \bigcirc = \bigcirc\bigcirc\bigcirc\bigcirc$

Each member is composed of the same four digits. What are the numbers?

43. The reversal of a seven-digit number exceeds 6 times the number by 246919. What is the number?

44. For certain army manoeuvres preliminary tests were made round a circuit of roads, having a whole number of miles, less than 45, in length. Two

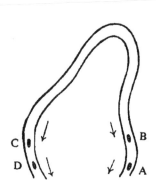

trucks, A and B, travel steadily at rates of 36 and 60 miles per hour respectively, clockwise. Two motorcycles with side-cars, C and D, travel in the opposite direction at speeds of 25 and 50 miles per hour, respectively. They manoeuvre till all four are abreast at an instant taken as the starting time. After that, every time C passes A a message is thrown into the side-car, which is then tossed into B on passing. Similarly, every time D passes B a message is thrown into the side-car, which is then tossed into A on passing. At exactly noon an air-view photo showed part of the road with all four vehicles as indicated, after B had overtaken and passed A three times, and a certain number of messages had been delivered. It was noted that at that moment C was a fraction under 5 miles from B and that 60 seconds after the picture was taken B arrived at the point where A is shown. The questions are:

a) How many miles in the circuit?
b) At what time did they start?
c) What was the starting point?
d) How many messages did C deliver?
e) How many messages did D deliver?

45. Number Detecting. Bill Jones, the car conductor, was brought up before the District Inspector in the Main Office and asked to tell what he knew of certain thefts from the lockers during the past year. He explained that he knew who had done it, but had refrained from informing since the man had left along with a lot of others shortly after Jones had found him out.

"Who was he?" asked the Inspector.

"I don't know his name... Tom Something-or-other."

"What can you tell us about him? What was his number?"

"I don't know that. Yet, it's funny. He was always calculating percentages and things. I heard him say he could remember his number by multiplying his house number by his recently married cousin's age, and that gave it. He said it was queer how the ten figures of the three numbers were all different."

"Do you remember anything else—about his number, for instance?"

"No, except that I believe the figure 8 to be lucky, especially if it is in the middle of a number. His middle figure wasn't an 8. That's all I know."

"And that's a great help," said the Inspector, sarcastically.

The next day Bill was called in again. The Inspector spoke: "I have finally found the man's badge number, but am in doubt about his house number. I have learned he has two cousins, and have rough estimates of their ages. Tell me: Was the cousin he spoke of a man or a woman?"

"A man."

"Ah, yes, the elder of the two. Good! I now know his house number."

What was the man's house number, and what was his badge number?

·

III   GEOMETRY

The distinction between a mathematical puzzle and a mathematical problem is not very definite. Let us say simply that the latter is subject to the immediate application of mathematical technique and presupposes some degree of technical knowledge, whereas the former is not directly subject to such technical application and presupposes but a minimum of technical knowledge.

One-way paths

In this spirit let us regard a network of one-way paths going from X to Y, where we desire to know the total number of such distinct paths. (In discussing this, we are encroaching on the subject matter of Chapter VII.) If we let the other letters represent the number of distinct ways of arriving at them from X, we have, clearly, $A = B = 1$.

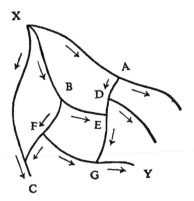

Also, $D=A=1$, whence $E=B+D=2$. Similarly, $F = B = 1, C = 1 + F = 2$, and $G = E + F = 3$. In each case the total number of ways of reaching a point is the sum of the ways of reaching all the points which join it immediately preceding. It is quite obvious that this procedure will give the total number at Y, regardless of the complexity of the array. (See Ex. 19.)

It may be noted that this procedure may be reversed, starting at Y.

Lattice points

Suppose we have an array of m × n lattice points (m ⩾ n) and inquire how many sets of four of these points will form a square.

Suppose, first, that the squares have sides parallel to the sides of the array. Starting with a 1 × 1 in the upper left corner, we note that that square can be moved to the right to m — 2 additional positions. Further, this row of m — 1 squares can be moved downward to n — 2 additional positions, giving a total of (m — 1)(n — 1) unit squares. Following the same procedure, we have a total of (m — 2)(n — 2) squares two units wide. The largest square is clearly n — 1 units wide. We then sum up the product (m — k)(n — k) for all values of k from 1 to n — 1 to get the total of squares with sides parallel to those of the array. This sum is $(n - 1)n(3m - n - 1)/6$.

We have now to consider squares with sides on the bias, like the one shown. Clearly each is enclosed in a square of the type we have already counted. The dimensions of the latter square are $a + b$, where a and b are the sides of the triangles having the sides of the oblique square as hypotenuses. The number of such squares we have already seen to be $(m - a - b)$ $(n - a - b)$. We have then to sum up this expression for all non-zero values of a and b subject to the condition that $a + b \geqslant n - 1$. This turns out to be

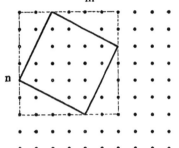

$$(n - 1)n(n + 1)(2m - n)/12.$$

For a square array, $m = n$, and the number of squares is

$$(n - 1)n^2(n + 1)/12.$$

Two difficult problems

It is difficult to specify just how far-reaching a chosen method of procedure may be. If happily chosen it may solve problems that would otherwise baffle the skilled mathematician. Indeed, one conscious procedure of the skilled mathematician is to hunt for a point of view, or a method of attack, from which or with which a problem can readily be resolved. At times the method used is selected quite accidentally from innumerable other methods of approach. At times such a method shows up with unusual power in a certain direction. This is seen in the "by-products" of many investigations. A simple special case of such, with scaffolding removed, may offer a very difficult problem to those not familiar with the particular method of procedure adopted. The hitting upon such a method is often a matter of pure chance. However, the mathematician, like the more material scientist, must be an opportunist, ready to seize upon any such revealed power and sense its possibilities. Thus there is no telling in advance just how difficult a problem will be. Someone may turn up with a method of procedure which just fits that problem, whereupon the problem becomes "ancient history". However, two of the exercises appended hereto suggest problems which, to the writer, offer questions of real difficulty. Given a rectangle with commensurable sides, $m \times n$, what is the fewest number of squares into which it can be divided? (See Ex. 14.) Again (see Ex. 15), given the integer n, and a chosen unit of length, what is the minimum area which can be cut up into n rectangles so that the 2n dimensions of these rectangles

37

shall be different integers? For $n = 1$, the answer is 1×2. For $n = 2$, or $n = 3$, or $n = 4$ there is no solution. Is there one for $n = 6$? The writer has not even tried to find out. Doubtless that is not difficult, but then the general theorem looms up. The problem may be made still more difficult by requiring that all the dimensions (possibly even including the whole rectangle) be different primes.

A generalization of Ex. 18 also forms a difficult problem. Here the first difficulty would be the matter of classifying networks in some way that would be effective for analysis.

Some geometrical lacunae

The student of mathematics would do well to review the elements, and put his finger on inaccuracies, incomplete arguments or other lacunae in the material presented. Let us examine one or two here:

Consider the problem; given the altitudes of a triangle, a, b, c, construct the triangle.

The usual solution offered is quite neat, but incomplete: Suppose the sides of the triangle to be x, y, z. Then

$$ax = by = cz.$$

Now form a triangle with a, b, c as the sides. Let its altitudes by u, v, w. Then

$$au = bv = cw,$$

whence

$$\frac{u}{x} = \frac{v}{y} = \frac{w}{z}.$$

The triangle formed with u, v, w as sides is then similar to the one with x, y, z as sides, and the solution is quite readily completed.

The point here is that we are asked to form a triangle with the altitudes given as sides. Now that may not be possible. For example, suppose the altitudes are 3, 4, 10. At once we are thwarted, and the solution offered fails.

Of course, a general solution is readily found: Take any arbitrary length, X. Then find Y so that $aX = bY$. Then find Z so that $bY = cZ$. Then $aX = bY = cZ$ and

$$\frac{X}{x} = \frac{Y}{y} = \frac{Z}{z},$$

and the solution is then completed as before.

38

The point of the matter is simply this; x, y, z are not *any* lengths. We must have $z < x + y$. Now

$$\frac{x}{\frac{1}{a}} = \frac{y}{\frac{1}{b}} = \frac{z}{\frac{1}{c}},$$

whence

$$\frac{1}{c} < \frac{1}{a} + \frac{1}{b} = \frac{a + b}{ab},$$

or

$$c > \frac{ab}{a + b}.$$

Again, let us consider a problem by G. Y. Sosnow which appeared in the American Mathematical Monthly for March 1926.

Before doing so, however, let us review a simple theorem; that the shortest distance from a point A to a straight line QR and then to a point B on the same side of QR is a broken line making equal angles with the straight line in question. Let P be the reflection of A in QR, and draw BP cutting QR in Q. Draw AQ. Clearly, AQ and BQ make equal angles with QR. Further, if R be any other point on QR, PR + BR > PB, whence AR + BR > PB, or > AQ + QB.

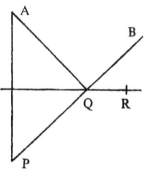

The problem in question is to prove the theorem that if we drop perpendiculars from the intersection of the diagonals of a cyclic quadrilateral to the four sides and connect the feet of these in order, we have a quadrilateral of minimum perimeter inscribed in the given cyclic quadrilateral.

Let ABCD be *any* quadrilateral and EFGH a quadrilateral of minimum perimeter inscribed in it. Now HE and FE must make equal angles with AB, else another point, E', can be found on AB, so that HE' + FE' < HE + FE. Similarly, the other sides of EFGH meeting a side of ABCD make equal angles with it. This we have indicated by the repetition of the Greek letters. Now

$$\alpha + \delta + A = 180°,$$
$$\beta + \gamma + C = 180°.$$
$$A + C = 360° - (\alpha + \beta + \gamma + \delta).$$

Also, $\beta + \alpha + B = 180°,$
               $\delta + \gamma + D = 180°,$
whence $B + D = 360° - (\alpha + \beta + \gamma + \delta)$
               $= A + C.$

In other words, if a quadrilateral EFGH of minimum perimeter inscribed

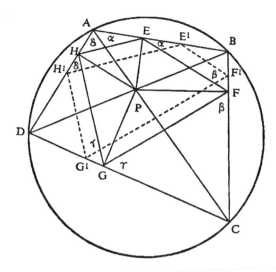

in ABCD in the manner indicated exists, ABCD *must be cyclic*. The requirement that ABCD be cyclic is then redundant.

Again, let ABCD be cyclic and EFGH an inscribed quadrilateral of minimum perimeter. Take another point E′ on AB, draw E′F′∕∕EF, then E′H′∕∕EH and F′G′∕∕FG, and connect G′H′.

Quite obviously, the perpendiculars from E to H′E′ and E′ to EF are equal. Hence, in sequence, the perpendicular from H′ on GH equals that from H on H′E′, which equals that from E on H′E′, which equals that from E′ on EF, which equals that from F′ on EF, which equals that from F on F′G′, which equals that from G on F′G′, which equals that from G′ on GH. Hence G′H′ is parallel to GH. Further, the perimeter E′F′G′H′ equals that of EFGH. Hence if one inscribed quadrilateral of minimum perimeter exists, an infinite number exist.

The question then arises, suppose the given quadrilateral ABCD is *not* cyclic, and an inscribed quadrilateral of minimum perimeter is required. What then? Without going into detail, the answer is that the required quadrilateral then degenerates into a triangle with one vertex at the junction of two of the sides of ABCD. Further, even this degenerate case may degenerate further, so that one side of this triangle shrinks to zero, and the required inscribed quadrilateral shrinks to a double diagonal of the given quadrilateral ABCD.

The essence of the latter question may be illustrated by the following problem: In the isosceles triangle ABC draw the shortest path from a point in AB to the line BC, then to the side AC.

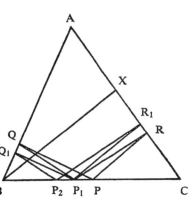

Let QPR be such a path. Then clearly $PQ \perp AB$ and $PR \perp AC$. Further, PQ and PR must make equal angles with BC, from which it follows that if such a path exists, the angles B and C are equal and the triangle *must* be isosceles. Moreover, in that case, P may be *any* point in the base. But what if ABC is not isosceles? Let $\angle B > \angle C$. PQ must be $\perp$ to AB and PR $\perp$ to AC. But then $\angle$ BPQ is less than $\angle$ CPR and we get a shorter path QP_1R by making the angles at the base equal. This path is further shortened if we take $P_1Q_1 \perp AB$ and $P_1R_1 \perp AC$. The path $Q_1P_1R_1$ is then again shortened if we replace P_1 by P_2, etc. Clearly, the limiting path is $BX \perp AC$.

An interesting elementary problem

This involves finding the diagonals of an inscribed quadrilateral in terms of the sides. Certain elementary texts show that $AC \cdot BD = ac + bd$. It is not too difficult to show that

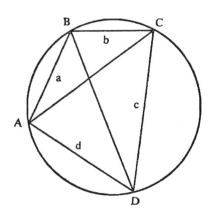

$$\frac{AC}{BD} = \frac{ad + bc}{ab + cd}.$$

This at once gives the values for AC and BD. From these we easily derive Heron's formula for the area of the inscribed quadrilateral,

$$\sqrt{(s - a)(s - b)(s - c)(s - d)},$$

where s is the semi-perimeter.

To the author it is very gratifying to find solutions to problems by elementary methods where one normally expects a highly technical treatment. It is in this spirit that a number of the

41

explanations in this book are offered. Incidentally, the writer has a strong predilection for solving algebraic problems by algebra, Euclidean problems by elementary geometry, etc. This of course does not preclude thinking of a proposition in other terms, getting enlightenment from other points of view or of combining results.

The problem we next deal with is a simple illustration of the power inherent in elementary mathematics.

A cut-up problem

We shall discuss cut-up problems in detail in Chapter VIII. However, a particular problem may be of interest to us here.

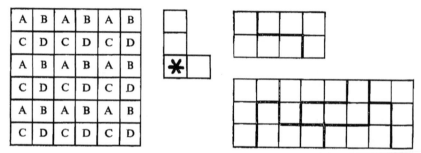

A	B	A	B	A	B
C	D	C	D	C	D
A	B	A	B	A	B
C	D	C	D	C	D
A	B	A	B	A	B
C	D	C	D	C	D

We have, for example, a rectangle 6×6 divided into 36 unit square cells as shown. Is it possible to cut this area into L's of the type shown, each consisting of 4 unit cells which may occur in any one of 8 possible orientations? We shall consider the more general case of a rectangle m by n, with mn unit cells.

The question arose from an attempt to explain Ex. 99 of Ch. VIII. If we use x L's and y Greek Crosses the total number of cells involved would be $4x + 5y = 36$. Here y must be a multiple of 4. It cannot be twice 4. It could be 4. Could it be 0? Then we would have $x = 9$. Several trials raised the suspicion that that was impossible. In the effort to test that, the following demonstration was applied:

Clearly $m > 1$, $n > 1$, and mn is a multiple of 4. Suppose first that m and n are both even and each twice an odd number. Let us mark the first row of cells alternately with the letters A and B, the second alternately with the letters C and D, the third again with A and B, etc.

Now let the corner cell of the L, with the asterisk, fall on an A square x times, on a B square y times, on a C square z times, on a D square t times. (It will be noted that the possibility of any of these numbers being 0 will not vitiate the argument.) In the first case we have x instances where 2 A cells are covered, one B cell, one C cell, and no D cell.

42

Following this procedure, we have then:

x cases covering 2 A, 1 B, 1 C, 0 D cells;
y cases covering 1 A, 2 B, 0 C, 1 D cells;
z cases covering 1 A, 0 B, 2 C, 1 D cells;
t cases covering 0 A, 1 B, 1 C, 2 D cells.

Now the total number of A cells is mn/4, an odd number. The same is true for the B, C and D cells. Hence

$$2x + y + z = mn/4$$
$$x + 2y + t = mn/4$$
$$x + 2z + t = mn/4$$
$$y + z + 2t = mn/4.$$

From the first two equations (or the last two),

$$2x + 2y + (x + y + z + t) = 2mn/4,$$

an even number.

Hence $x + y + z + t$ is an even number. But that is the total number of L's to be had, and must be mn/4, an odd number. Hence in this case the dissection is impossible.

Suppose now mn/4 is still odd, but m (say) is odd, and n 4 times an odd number. The procedure is identical except that the equations we have found have $(m + 1)n/4$ or $(m - 1)n/4$ on the right. We conclude then that the dissection is impossible in this case too.

Suppose now mn as a multiple of 8. If m and n are both even, we can cut the entire array into blocks 4×2. As seen in the figure, each of these can be cut into 2 L's in 2 ways. Suppose now m (say) is odd, and n a multiple of 8. Here m is at least 3 and can be cut into two parts, one even and the other 3. The first permits of cuts into 2×4's. The second part leaves a strip 3 by n, and can be cut into blocks 3×8. Again, as shown in the figure, each of these can be cut into 6 L's. Hence in this case there is always a solution.

So it follows that a necessary and sufficient condition for the rectangle to be cut into L's is that m > 1, n > 1, and mn be divisible by 8.

Another elementary problem

The author's solution of a problem given him some years ago may be of interest here:

Let A be the mid-point of the chord BC, and PQ and RS any two other chords through A. Draw PR cutting BC in X and SQ cutting BC in Y. To prove $XA = AY$. Take T on PR (or PR produced) so that $\angle PAT = \angle SYA$. Now $\angle APT = \angle YSA$. $\therefore \triangle s$ PAT and SYA are similar.

$$\therefore \frac{PT}{SA} = \frac{TA}{AY} = \frac{AP}{YS}.$$

43

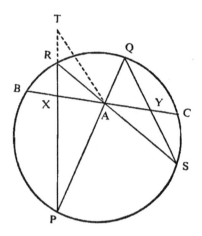

The $\triangle$s XAR and XTA are also similar. Hence

$$\frac{XA}{XT} = \frac{AR}{TA} = \frac{RX}{AX}, \text{ whence } \frac{AR}{AY} = \frac{RX \cdot AP}{AX \cdot YS}.$$

In quite similar fashion we obtain,

$$\frac{AQ}{AX} = \frac{QY \cdot SA}{AY \cdot PX}, \text{ whence}$$

$$\frac{AR \cdot QY \cdot SA}{AY \cdot AY \cdot PX} = \frac{AQ \cdot RX \cdot AP}{AX \cdot AX \cdot YS}, \text{ or } \frac{(AR \cdot SA)(QY \cdot YS)}{AY^2} = \frac{(AQ \cdot AP)(RX \cdot PX)}{AX^2}.$$

Let $BA = AC = a$. Then

$$QY \cdot YS = BY \cdot YC = (a + AY)(a - AY) = a^2 - AY^2,$$
$$RX \cdot XP = BX \cdot XC = (a + XA)(a - XA) = a^2 - XA^2;$$
$$AR \cdot SA = AQ \cdot AP = a^2.$$

$$\therefore \quad \frac{a^2(a^2 - AY^2)}{AY^2} = \frac{a^2(a^2 - XA^2)}{XA^2},$$

whence $XA = AY$.

A different type of lacuna here is the fact that the lines QR and PS also intersect BC (produced) in points equidistant from A. A slight modification of the method used will serve for that case also.

44

The Fermat Point

Given a triangle ABC, the Fermat Point is a point in its plane where

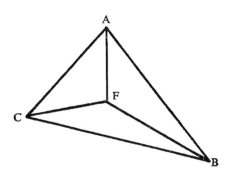

the sum of its distances from the vertices is a minimum. It is possible to analyse the figure with the use of very elementary steps so as to determine the position of F in any particular case. The statement the writer has seen that F is the point common to the three circles having the three sides of ABC as chords and including angles of 60° externally is not always correct. However, we shall omit the details here.

An interesting modification is to find F so that FB + FC − FA is a minimum. This also the author has analysed, but has found it necessary at one point to utilize the calculus.

A novel method

An amusing recreation is to take some interesting geometric figure and worry it threadbare. A good example is the following, where some of the theorems are to be found in Casey's "A Sequel to Euclid" and Altshiller-Court's "College Geometry":

Let $A_1A_2A_3$ be any triangle. With each of the sides as a base construct an equilateral triangle outwardly. Let $A_1A_2B_3$ be typical of these, with circumcenter C_3. Also construct equilateral triangles inwards. Of these let $A_1A_2b_3$, with circumcenter c_3, be typical. Then, in order, the following may be proved:

1. The three outer circles intersect in a common point P.
2. The three lines A_iB_i are equal.
3. These three lines pass through P.
4. The three inner circles intersect in a common point Q.
5. The three lines A_ib_i are equal.
6. These three lines pass through Q.
7. The triangle $C_1C_2C_3$ is equilateral.
8. The triangle $c_1c_2c_3$ is equilateral.
9. $PA_1 \perp C_2C_3$, etc.
10. $QA_1 \perp c_2c_3$, etc.
11. The six triangles $A_1C_3c_2$, $A_1C_2c_3$, etc. are all equal and similar to the given triangle A.

45

12. The quadrilaterals $A_1c_2C_1c_3$ are parallelograms.
13. The quadrilaterals $A_1C_3c_1C_2$ are parallelograms.
14. $Pc_1 \perp PA_1$ and $\parallel C_2C_3$.
15. $QC_1 \perp QA_1$ and $\parallel c_2c_3$.
16. $c_1c_2c_3$ P is cyclic.
17. $C_1C_2C_3$ Q is cyclic.
18. Apart from P and Q, the six circumcircles mentioned intersect only on the sides, or sides produced, of the given triangle.
19. The sum of the squares of the sides of the two equilateral triangles C and c is equal to the sum of the squares of the sides of the original triangle.
20. The difference of the areas of the two equilateral triangles C and c is equal to the area of the given triangle.

More relations are readily found. However, the diagram soon gets confusing, with but little paper left visible. We shall give a proof of the last item. Though the theorem was published in the American Mathematical Monthly (see AMM for March 1929, p. 169), the method used to derive it was not given. We deem it of interest for its own sake, so shall indicate it briefly:

Let a line forming a closed circuit represent the area within. If the boundary is traced with the area to the left it shall be deemed positive, if on the right negative. If a moving point completes a closed loop and moves on, the closed area shall be taken with proper sign (that is, accounted positive if the enclosed area is to the left of the directed boundary, as traced by the moving point, negative if to the right of the tracing point) and added to the area of the figure finally completed. In this case we shall trace only broken-line circuits.

With the convention adopted, we have then the formal relation

$$AB ---- PQR ---- A = AB ---- PQRPR ---- A$$
$$= AB ---- PR ---- A + PQRP.$$

We may now attack our problem.

Since PA_3 is bisected by the line of centres C_1C_2, $C_2PC_1 = P_1A_3C_2$, etc. Hence, representing the areas of the principal triangles by their common letters, the hexagon formed by the vertices of A and C is equal to 2C:

$$2C = A_1C_3A_2C_1A_3C_2A_1.$$

Now the triangles outside the A triangle have the sum 2C-A. Remembering that $A_1c_2A_3C_2$ is a parallelogram, that the area of this is bisected by A_3A_1, we have, on subtracting these three outer triangles from A

$$2A-2C = A_1c_3A_2c_1A_3c_2A_1 = c_3A_2c_1A_3c_2A_1c_3$$
$$= c_3c_1c_2c_3 + c_3A_2c_1c_3 + c_1A_3c_2c_1 + c_2A_1c_3c_2.$$

Again, since $c_1A_2c_3C_2$ is a parallelogram bisected by c_1c_3

$$2A\text{-}2C = c_3c_1c_2c_3 + c_1C_2c_3c_1 + c_2C_3c_1c_2 + c_3C_1c_2c_3.$$

Now

$$C = C_2PC_1C_2 + C_3PC_2C_3 + C_1PC_3C_1,$$

or

$$C_1C_2C_3C_1 = C_2c_3C_1C_2 + C_3c_1C_2C_3 + C_1c_2C_3C_1,$$
$$0 = C_1C_2C_3C_1 + C_1c_3C_2C_1 + C_2c_1C_3C_2 + C_3c_2C_1C_3$$
$$= C_1c_3C_2c_1C_3c_2C_1 = c_3C_2c_1C_3c_2C_1c_3$$
$$= c_3c_1c_2c_3 + c_3C_2c_1c_3 + c_1C_3c_2c_1 + c_2C_1c_3c_2,$$

whence

$$c_1C_2c_3c_1 + c_2C_3c_1c_2 + c_3C_1c_2c_3 = c_3c_1c_2c_3.$$

We have then

$$2A - 2C = 2c_3c_1c_2c_3.$$

We now note that if A and C are traced anticlockwise C is traced clockwise—that is, $c_3c_1c_2c_3 = -c$.

Hence

$$A = C - c.$$

Comments on Exercises

9. There are two minimum paths, totalling twice a diagonal.

20. It would be well to letter the individual triangles comprising the figure and take combinations of these.

21. The results of this are subject to check by Euler's Formula.

23. The strokes may be straight or circular.

24. If AB > CD, lay off AE = CD on AB. Draw the perpendicular bisector FG of EB at F. With E as centre and AF as radius draw an arc cutting FG in G. Consider FG.

25. Given to me through a classmate in preparatory school, with a promised cash prize for the solution (I solved the problem, but never got the prize!).

27. See AMM for March 1929, p. 169.

Exercises

1. Interchange two pairs of numbers, then draw a line across the face of the clock so that the sum of the numbers on either side of it shall have a 0 in units place.

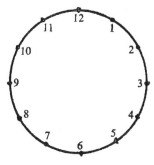

2. (Mental arithmetic.) If the volume of the earth were added to that of the sun, approximately how much would be added to the sun's radius?

3.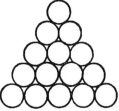

a) How many distinct triangles may be traced in the first figure?

b) How many distinct triangles may be formed by selecting triads of dots from the second figure?

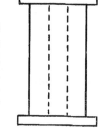

4. How many barrels need be shifted in order to have a similar array with the apex pointing in the opposite direction?

5. An equilateral triangle of under 30″ to a side is composed of triangular tiles 1″ to a side. To make room for a post, an inner triangle is removed and these tiles are used to fill out a border exactly to an enlarged triangle. What are the dimensions of the three triangles referred to?

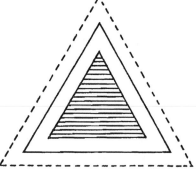

6. Assuming:

a) The Earth is 8000 miles in diameter;

b) the Sun is 93000000 miles away;

c) the Sun's visual angle is half a degree. Compute the relative volumes by simple arithmetic.

7. A roll of paper 10″ thick consists of 350 turns about a wooden core 2″ thick. Approximately what is the total length of the unwound paper?

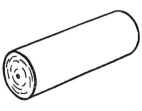

8. Steel wire with a square cross-section $\frac{1}{16}″ \times \frac{1}{16}″$ is wound snugly round a metal spool to a total thickness of 4″. The core of the spool is 1″ and the distance between the flanges is 8″. Approximately how many yards of wire are on the spool?

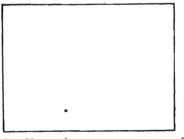

9. Given a point within a rectangle. What is the minimum distance from that point to each of the four sides and back again?

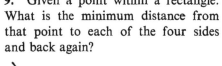

10. Two mirrors meet at an angle greater than 90°. Can one, within the angle, ever see himself by double reflection?

11. A goldsmith was commissioned to construct a closed box of given volume on a square base, using gold sheets of required thickness and fineness. A mathematical friend assured him that a cube with that volume would consume the least material. Later on the man was commissioned to construct an open box. His mathematical friend was not available. How, with just ordinary common sense, could he decide the proportion of height to width?

12. How may these four blocks be arranged so as to enclose the maximum area?

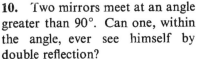

13. Leaving the 12 in position, move five of the numbers so as to have the sums of alternate sets each 39; also, so that a line through the centre in each of three positions has the sum of the numbers on either side 39.

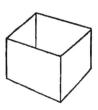

14. Show how to divide a rectangle 13 × 11 into the fewest number of whole squares.

49

15. Find a rectangle of the minimum area which can be cut into five rectangles with integral sides so that the ten dimensions of these five rectangles shall all be different. (A given unit of length is presupposed.)

16. a) How many distinct squares may be traced in the first figure?

b) How many distinct sets of four dots each forming a square may be selected from the second figure? (See S.M. June 1948, p. 165.)

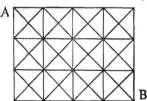

17. In Ex. 16, how many rectangles are there in the first figure?

18. In Ex. 16, how many rectangles are there in the second figure?

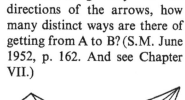

19. Travelling only in the directions of the arrows, how many distinct ways are there of getting from A to B? (S.M. June 1952, p. 162. And see Chapter VII.)

20. 1) How many distinct polygons are formed by a selection of these 15 line segments?

2) Which line segment is to be removed so that the remaining figure will yield the fewest polygons? (S.M. for March 1953, pp. 79/80.)

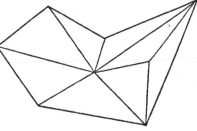

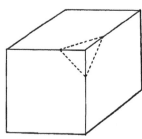

21. Shaving the Cube. We start with a cube. Then:

1) Divide each edge into three;

2) connect these so as form tetrahedra at each vertex;

3) cut off each such tetrahedron;

4) apply the same operation to the new figure;

5) then apply the same operation to the last, getting a fourth figure.

a) How many vertices are there in the last figure?

b) How many edges are there in the last figure?

c) How many faces are there in the last figure?

d) If the operation be repeated successively, how many of each of these are there in the nth figure?

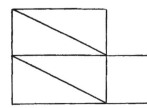

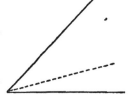

22. Arrange these five pieces so as to form a square. (Cf. Chapter VIII.)

23. Two lines meet so as to form an angle. In how few strokes may one obtain one-fourth of this angle?

24. Two lengths are given. In how few strokes may one find their mean proportional?

25. Construct a triangle; given the altitude, the bisector of the vertical angle and the median to the base.

A	B	A	B	A	B	A	B	A
C	D	C	D	C	D	C	D	C
A	B	A	B	A	B	A	B	A
C	D	C	D	C	D	C	D	C
A	B	A	B	A	B	A	B	A
C	D	C	D	C	D	C	D	C
A	B	A	B	A	B	A	B	A
C	D	C	D	C	D	C	D	C
A	B	A	B	A	B	A	B	A

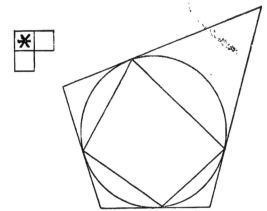

26. Following the method of the text, show that if the 9 × 9 block shown be cut into 3-celled L's of the kind shown, the cell with the asterisk will fall on an A 11 times, on a D twice, and on a B or C seven times each.

27. Analyse thoroughly the figure formed by a circle, any circumscribed quadrilateral, and the inscribed quadrilateral with vertices at the points of tangency of the sides of the first.

IV   LETTER DIVISIONS

In this type of puzzle, or game, sometimes called CRYPTIC DIVISIONS or, more generally, CRYPTARITHMS, an ordinary long division is first carried out. Then the division is put in code form by placing some definite letter for each 1 in the division, some other specific letter for each 2, etc. The problem then is for someone to reconstruct the division from the clues inherent in the arrangement of the figures as indicated by the letters which represent them. For example, suppose we start with the following division:

```
7 4 9 ) 5 0 4 2 6 4 ( 6 7 3
        4 4 9 4
        ─────────
        5 4 8 6
        5 2 4 3
        ─────────
          2 4 3 4
          2 2 4 7
          ─────────
            1 8 7
```

Suppose now we make our substitution according to the following scheme:

```
0   1   2   3   4   5   6   7   8   9
A   E   I   H   D   B   F   J   G   C   .
```

We get this coded arrangement:

```
J D C ) B A D I F D ( F J H
        D D C D
        ─────────
        B D G F
        B I D H
        ─────────
          I D H D
          I I D J
          ─────────
            E G J.
```

Very often, as in marking sales prices on merchandise, for the salesman's private information an ordinary word or name of 10 different letters is used as a mnemonic. This type of puzzle offers a fine exercise in logic applied to figures. When played as a game, two or more people exchange such divisions, the first to solve getting a point.

Typical analysis

Let us now refer to the coded division, and let us assume that we do not know where it came from. How can we deduce the original code from the array? We shall first make a number of simple observations based on this particular puzzle, but it will be observed that the methods are universally applicable. We suggest the reader follow the reasoning with pad and pencil.

1. The four-digit number DDCD added to the three-digit number BDG equals BADI. Similarly, BIDH added to IDH gives BDGF, etc.

2. DDCD divided by F gives JDC;
DDCD divided by JDC gives F; etc.

3. J must be greater than any of the leading digits D, B, I, E in the four-digit partial products or the three-digit remainder.

4. Since all these digits are different, and no leading digit can be 0, J must be at least 5.

5. From the first subtraction, B must be 1 more than D.

6. From the second subtraction, D must be twice I or, if 1 is to be carried, 1 more than twice I. Hence I is at most 4.

7. From the last subtraction, since J is more than D, twice J must be 10 more than D. Hence again J is at least 5.

8. We have ten different digits: A, B, C, D, E, F, G, H, I, J. One of these must be 0. For quite obvious reasons, all but A cannot be 0. For example, G is not 0 because, in the first subtraction, D and I would have to be the same. We conclude then that, by elimination of the others in like manner, A must be 0.

9. In the first subtraction, D is under D. Hence C must be 0 or 9. But C cannot be 0 since A is 0. Hence C is 9.

10. In the first subtraction (or, for convenience, the corresponding addition), since A is 0, and 1 is to be carried, D plus B must be 9.

11. F must be greater than D. (Similarly, J is greater than B, H is greater than I, etc.). Since B is the next larger to D, F must be greater than B.

12. From the last addition, since there is 1 to carry, D plus G plus 1 is either H or 10 more than H. But, from the first subtraction, D plus G is either I or 10 plus I, that is, the sum ends in I. Hence I plus 1 is the same as H.

13. From the last subtraction, D must be even. Hence, in the preceding subtraction, or addition, there cannot be anything to carry in the 1 place, and D must be exactly twice I.

14. Since D plus G ends in I (first subtraction), and D is twice I, I plus G must be 10.

15. Since twice I is D, and twice J is 10 plus D, J must be 5 more than I.

16. Since the leading figure, B, of the second partial product is greater

than the leading figure, D, of the first, the corresponding multiplier, J, of the quotient must be greater than F.

17. From item 14, since 1 is at most 4, G must be greater than I.

18. Now I is less than D. Hence H, which is next larger than I, must also be less than D. So in the last addition there must be 1 to carry over the H, and D must be equal to 1 plus E plus 1. But D is twice I. Hence I must be 1 more than E.

19. B is D plus 1. Since D is twice I, B is twice I plus 1. Since E is 1 less than I, B is twice E plus 3. Hence B is at least 5. Hence F is at least 6. Since J is still greater, J is at least 7. Since 9 is already accounted for, F must be 6 or 7 and J 7 or 8.

20. But in the second subtraction F is shown to be *even*. Hence F must be 6. Since D is even, and less than F, and is equal to I plus E plus 1, D must be 4. Hence B is 5. From item 13, J must be 7. Since H is less than D, and F is 6, the second subtraction shows H to be 3. The last subtraction shows G to be 8. Hence I is 2 and E is 1.

This solves the particular problem. Of course, we could solve this problem without actually noting each of the items we have mentioned. That is done to illustrate the method. For example, from Item 10, B plus D is 9. But B is D plus 1. Hence D is 4, B is 5, etc. Also of course, in actually working out such a problem, the conclusions are not written down in such a formal way. If, for example, F is shown to be either 6 or 7, these tentative values are written in small figures under it. Similarly, if J is anywhere from 5 to 9, these five possibilities may be put under the J in the quotient, and individual figures crossed out one by one as they are found to be untenable.

Other tactics are often serviceable. We may mention several. But if the problem is really difficult, and one is willing to go through the labour, it is effective to choose an important digit, say the units of the divisor, and consider 9 separate problems according as each possibility from 1 to 9 is assumed for that digit. Even so, having shown it must be, say, 7, if the problem is still hard, it may be subdivided similarly by doing the same for another important digit.

If the units digit of the divisor is 1, each partial product must have a units digit the same as the corresponding figure of the quotient. Suppose the units figure of the divisor is P, a digit of the quotient is Q, and the corresponding product ends in Q. If P is seen not to be 1, then either Q is 5 and P is odd, or P is 6 and Q is even. Again, we note that five of the digits (including 0) must be even, the other five odd. If, as a result of a tentative assumption, it follows that *six* different digits must be even, or odd, then that assumption is untenable. For instance, in the last example, suppose we assume C to be even. We have A even. Also, from the products and additions, D, H, J, F must also be even. But six even digits are impossible. Hence C must be odd. Obviously, C cannot be 1. Also, since D, the unit of a partial product is different from both C and from 0, C cannot be 5. Hence C is restricted to the numbers 3, 7, 9! Of course, we have seen otherwise that C must be 9. But the device above about the evenness or oddness of a key figure is very effective. Again, having determined that C is 9, note that on pairing digits of the quotient and corresponding units digits of the partial products, the sum must be 10. For example, F plus D is 10, J plus H is 10, etc.

Special devices

Very often special devices work quickly. Incidentally, it is always well to remember the writer's dictum, 'Anything queer is a clue'. The most difficult kind of puzzle is one where there is nothing irregular, nothing 'to get hold of'. Consider the following example:

```
e f ) e i  d g h ( g j e
      c c c
      ─────
      c f g
      b g a
      ─────
        b e h
        b h j
        ─────
          b i
```

Here there is something queer; the product *ccc*. Let us get hold of that. Now *ccc* is *c* times 111. But 111 is 3 times 37. But *ccc* results from the multiplication of *ef* by the single digit *g*. This single digit cannot contain the factor 37. Hence 37 must be contained in *ef*. Hence *ef* is either 37 or 74 But, as we have seen, *e* is greater than each of the different digits *c*, *b*. Further, since in the first addition there is 1 to carry, *c* must be greater than *i*. Hence *e* is also greater than *i*, which, from the last subtraction, is not 0. Hence *e* is greater than each of three different digits none of which is 0. Hence *e* is at least 4. Therefore *ef* cannot be 37—that is, *ef* must be 74. This at once solves the problem.

Again, let us look at the following:

```
E H B ) G C B J 1 E ( J F C
        B E E B
        ───────
        H J F I
        H J F E
        ───────
          H E
```

Here the queer item is the product BEEB. Now this number is made up of B times 1001 plus E times 110. Since 1001 is divisible by 11, the whole number also is. Hence the divisor must be divisible by 11. So E plus B is H or 11 more than H. Since E is seen to be greater than H, E plus B equals H plus 11. Also, since J times B ends in B, either B is 5 and J is odd, or J is 6 and B is even. Since, as we have already noted in an earlier paragraph, B is not 5, we must have J equal to 6 and B even. Further, C must be 0. As J is greater than B, B is 2 or 4. But E is even. Also E must be 4 or 8. Since E plus B exceeds H by 11, we must have E = 8 and B = 4, whence G is 5. From the first multiplication, H is 1. This makes F 2 and I 9.

Another device is to combine the order of precedence. For example, in our first problem, we noted that B is D plus 1, H is I plus 1, I is E plus 1, D is greater than I, etc. We have then the following tentative sequential arrangement of these digits:

$$— — E\ I\ H — — D\ B — —.$$

We then move the blocks of letters either way a space or two at a time, according to our findings, until only one possible position is left. The rest is then filled in easily.

Application to other types of problem

Of course this type of problem is not restricted to divisions. Many interesting types have been prepared, using additions, multiplications, square roots, fractions, etc. In analysis, the same principles apply.

We take up two problems which are amenable to this method. Both are solved from other points of view elsewhere in this book. Consider the following problem (Cf. Ch. 1 and Ex. 15, Ch. II):

> On multiplying a certain six-digit number by 6 we get another six-digit number. The new number consists of the same digits as the original number, but with an interchange of the two adjoining triads of digits of which it is composed. What is the number?

Let us write the computation in the following form:

1	4		8	5	
A	B	C	D	E	F
	34			56	
					6
8	5		1	4	
D	E	F	A	B	C
	56			34	

First the letters of the computation are written down. (Let the reader follow this on a separate sheet of paper.) Obviously, A must be 1. D is at least 6. Now, on multiplying by 6, the most we have to carry is 5. If D in the upper line is assumed to be 7, since the number below is 1 we should have to carry 9. This is impossible. Similarly, if D is 9, we should have to carry 7. Hence D can be only 6 or 8. Suppose we try them separately. First, let D be 6. The computation then looks like this:

1	1	6	6	8	6
A	B	C	D	E	F
					6

6	8	6	1	1	6
D	E	F	A	B	C

Here B in the upper line is either 0 or 1. On getting the 1 in the second number we have to carry 5 from 6 times E. Hence E is at least 8. So the B in the upper line must be 1. Now E in the upper line cannot be 9, because we should otherwise have to carry 7 to get the 1 below. Therefore E is 8, and there is 3 to carry. Thus F is 5 or 6. But when multiplying the C by 6 we get an even number, to which is carried 4, an even number. Consequently F would have to be even, or 6. So C would have to be 6. This is found to be impossible. Hence, if there is any solution at all, D must be 8. We now refer back to our original arrangement and enter an '8' over each D. Now 6 times D is 48. Thus there is 3 to carry. Accordingly E must be 5 or 6. Also 6 times B must give 2 to carry. Hence B is 3 or 4. B cannot be 3, because 6 times 3 is 18, leaving 7 or 8 to carry. Therefore B is 4. Now E cannot be 6, since 6 times 6 is 36, requiring 8 to be carried to get the 4 below the E. Thus E must be 5. But there is 4 to carry here. So F is 7 or 8. But there is 5, an odd number, to carry with 6 times C, an even number, so that F must be odd. Hence F must be 7 and C 2. We have then determined the digits if there is a solution. We try these, and find the solution correct: $142857 \times 6 = 857142$.

In this connection it would be an interesting exercise for the reader to determine what solutions, if any, exist when other digits are used as multipliers.

The other problem follows (Cf. Chapters II and X):

Having used up all his money, a man cashed at the bank a cheque he had received. After spending $2.10, he noticed that he had left twice the amount written on the cheque. He realized at once that this was due to the teller's inadvertently interchanging the dollars and cents. How much was the cheque for?

We shall put the problem in the form of an addition. Suppose we write the amount of the cheque in the form $AB.CD. Then the problem takes the following form:

```
   A   B   C   D
   A   B   C   D
       2   1   0
  ─────────────────
   C   D   A   B
```

Obviously, A cannot be greater than 4. Also, B in the sum must be even. Let us try the different even numbers for B, starting with 0. Let B be 0. Then D in the sum may be 2, 3, or 4—nothing else. But if D in the units column is one of these figures then B in the sum cannot be 0. Hence B is not 0. Next, suppose B to be 2. Then D in the sum must be 6, 7 or 8. But only 6 in the units position for D gives 2 for B in the sum. Thus if B is 2, D is 6. Hence there is nothing to carry on, adding the tens column. But that would make C less than A, whereas from the first column C must be greater than A. Hence B is not 2. Suppose now B is 4. Then from the second column D is 0, 1 or 2. But only 2 for D in the units column gives 4 for B in the sum, with nothing to carry. Hence the tens column has at most 1 to carry. So the second column cannot give 2 for D. That makes 4 for D untenable. Suppose next that B is 6. Then from the second column D is either 4, 5 or 6. But none of these in the units column can give 6 for B in the sum. Therefore B cannot be 6, and if there is a solution at all, B must be 8. Consequently for the second column D must be 8, 9 or 0. The units column shows that of these only 9 for D gives 8 for B in the sum. Hence D is 9. Further, since 1 is to be carried, A in the sum must be even. Similarly, C in the sum must be odd. Accordingly A is either 0, 2 or 4. If in the first column A is 0, C is 1. That will not fit the tens column. Neither will 4 for A fit this column. So A is 2 as the only remaining possibility, giving 5 for C. The sum of money specified on the cheque is then $28.59.

Various modifications of this type of mathematical play have been adopted. For example, two sets of letter codes have been employed in the same problem, using ten large letters and ten small letters. Otherwise a combination of cryptarithm and skeleton arrangement, as discussed in the next chapter, has been tried. A good example is the author's solution of a problem by A. A. Bennett in the AMM for December 1927, pp. 539-40.

Exercises

1. B F A) A G I J D H (C I C
        I E H I
       ─────────
       F B C D
       F C I J
       ─────────
    . A I A H
       I E H I
       ─────────
        A E A

2. T R B) D S B DA (B HR
       H N R
       ─────────
       B U N D
       B S A B
       ─────────
       U T E A
       U T H N
       ─────────
         E

3. F U T) A E F T L S (S A U
       A S E A
       ─────────
       A A A L
       ME R U
       ─────────
       R R MS
       R A F A
       ─────────
        S T M

4. L C A) T S L U M N E (O S O E
       T U T S
       ─────────
       C N C M
       C O E O
       ─────────
       T E S N
       T U T S
       ─────────
       N L L E
       N L T U
       ─────────
        C N

5. D I B) R A T R B E (I B A
       R D L L
       ─────────
       E A D B
       E I E Y
       ─────────
       E C L E
       E C L E

6. M P N) M O M P A M (T S I
       O T S I
       ─────────
       M M N A
       MO P P
       ─────────
       O L M M
       O L M M

7. E S O) O E P R O P (M P E
       O ME T
       ─────────
       ME O O
       MC T R
       ─────────
       U U P P
       U U P P

8. D I M E) N I C K E L S (C E N T
       D I M E
       ─────────
       S L MDE
       S E C I E
       ─────────
       I DCKL
       I KDL S
       ─────────
       I E C N S
       I DT DT
       ─────────
       C I S D

9. EIGHT) S I XT E E N (TWO
　　　　 HNWNE
　　　　 ─────
　　　　 O I N G E
　　　　 E I G H T
　　　　 ───────
　　　　 I G X T T N
　　　　 I G W X O E
　　　　 ─────────
　　　　 I N X T

10. SEVEN) F O U R T E E N (TWO
　　　　　 F E O R E F
　　　　　 ─────────
　　　　　 F E V R N E
　　　　　 E T WU N W
　　　　　 ─────────
　　　　　 T WV N O N
　　　　　 WO F E U R
　　　　　 ─────────
　　　　　 T T T S S

11. ABC) Z A Y R R R (X Y Z
　　　　 Z B C Z
　　　　 ─────
　　　　 Q P Q R
　　　　 Q C Z Q
　　　　 ─────
　　　　 B C Z R
　　　　 B C Z R

12. BEZ) D C N N E (R B O
　　　　 Z Z O
　　　　 ─────
　　　　 A B A N
　　　　 A A I A
　　　　 ─────
　　　　 A N O E
　　　　 A N O E

13. GEA) N R G S A T (R H E
　　　　 N T R E
　　　　 ─────
　　　　 O P P A
　　　　 O A O N
　　　　 ─────
　　　　 T O O T
　　　　 T S G O
　　　　 ─────
　　　　 N P A

14. BNYF) N B B N N G (B O
　　　　　 N F Q Y U
　　　　　 ───────
　　　　　 A O B A G
　　　　　 A N A G Y
　　　　　 ───────
　　　　　 U E N U

15. KIHJ) H K K J F I T (N K N
　　　　　 H I F O H
　　　　　 ───────
　　　　　 H A 1 O I
　　　　　 H F A F A
　　　　　 ───────
　　　　　 H N A K T
　　　　　 H I F O H
　　　　　 ───────
　　　　　 H H A M

16. AST) B E A D E U (F E D
　　　　 B F D S
　　　　 ─────
　　　　 C T C E
　　　　 C B T A
　　　　 ─────
　　　　 C E F U
　　　　 C E F U

17. (See Ex. 21, Ch. II.) What five-digit number is reversed on multi-plying by 4?

18. When is the square root of one Q U A C K exactly one U A C? Here the distinct letters do not necessarily represent different digits.

19. 　　 D T Y
　　　　 Y T D
　　　　 ─────
　　　　 A B R T
　　　　 Y R N E
　　　 B T E T
　　　 ───────
　　　 B E S Y D T

20. 　　 O H E
　　　　　 I S
　　　　 ─────
　　　　 R C I L
　　　　 Y L Y Y
　　　　 ─────
　　　　 Y T S C L

21. 　　 Y S T V I
　　　　　　 X Y
　　　　 ─────────
　　　　 E H H I U V
　　　　 V S O I E I
　　　　 ─────────
　　　　 V O U S O H V

60

22.
```
    MLAB
     STM
   -------
   TNEMT
   BASBA
   BOBTR
   -------
   BTEMTET
```

23.
```
    FAT
     KI
   ------
   KSOK
   TSK
   ------
   MKTK
    REF
   ------
   MMRR
```

24.
```
   ABCDEF
 ×      3
 --------
   BDFACE
```

25. EJI) HCFIBH (FDF
```
      HCBA
      -------
       HCBH
       HCBA
       -------
          G
```

26. TJWV) JZJZCC (GG
```
       JQXCW
       -------
       JQWQC
       JQXCW
       -------
        TGQ
```

27. ERK) RSSLO (HS
```
      RPFA
      ------
      AEEO
      AHSR
      ------
       AOL
```

28.
```
   EIGHT
   THREE
   NINE
   ------
   TWENTY
```

29.
```
   FIVE
   TWO
   ONE
   -----
   EIGHT
```

30. In the cheque problem, suppose that after spending 99 cents the man had left three times the amount of the cheque. How much was that?

31.
```
   BFSA
   ETC
   -------
   OUOUB
   OTTSC
   BOBOF
   -------
   BFBUDDB
```

32. TRB) DSBDA (BHR
```
       HNR
       ------
       BUND
       BSAB
       ------
        UTEA
        UTHN
        ------
          E
```

33. (See AMM for December 1925, p. 521.)
```
        ABCDE
   ×        X
   ----------
        EDCBA
```
Here A ≠ 0,
and X ≠ 1.

34.
```
   SEVEN
   THREE
   TWO
   ------
   TWELVE
```

35.
```
   ELEVEN
   SEVEN
   TWO
   ------
   TWENTY
```

36. Solve Ex. 41 of Ch. I. by the methods of this chapter.

37. Solve Ex. 43 of Ch. II. by the methods of this chapter.

38. (See Ex. 18, Ch. II.) What is the smallest number with units digit 7 in which moving this 7 to the leading position is equivalent to subtracting 1 and multiplying by 2?

39. A five-digit number is such that, if the middle digit be moved to the leading position, the resulting number multiplied by 2 and the product reduced by 2, we get the reversal of the number. What is the number?

40. $\dfrac{A}{T} + \dfrac{G\,O}{H\,M} = \dfrac{R\,H\,S}{I\,O\,G}$ Each fraction is in its lowest terms and the first two denominators have no common factor.

41. $\dfrac{I}{A\,S} + \dfrac{A\,R}{F\,X} = \dfrac{I\,G\,A}{U\,T\,E}$ The same conditions as in Ex. 36.

42. $\dfrac{A}{B} + \dfrac{C}{D} + \dfrac{E}{F} = A\,\dfrac{C\,C}{A\,G\,D}$ Each fraction on the left is proper and in its lowest terms. No two of the first three denominators have a common factor.

43. John has $3.75 more on his person than Jack. But if he had as many dollars as cents and as many cents as dollars he would have $3.51 less than four times what Jack has. How much has each?

44. In making out a bill under $100 in 1948, a bookkeeper inadvertently added in the date. The amount was then double what would be obtained if the dollars and cents of the correct amount were interchanged. How much was the correct amount?

45. A man gave his older son a cheque for an odd amount, under $100. His younger son also got a cheque, for a smaller amount, with the dollars and cents of the first interchanged. The difference between the two cheques was in the form $XX.YY. The sum of the cents on both cheques was $1.19. The younger son had an even number of cents. How much did each receive?

46. The sum of two six-digit numbers is 999999. Four times one of the numbers gives the reverse of the other. What are the numbers?

47. Four times either of two numbers gives the reverse of the other. Show that:

a) The numbers must be equal.

b) The smallest possible number is 2178.

c) Others are of the form 2199···9978.

48. Solve Ex. 52 of Ch. I by the methods of this chapter.

49. (See Ex. 33, Ch. II.) Transferring the units digit of a certain number to the leading position is equivalent to multiplying the number by 7. How many digits has the number? What numbers will serve?

V   SKELETON DIVISIONS

Explanation

In this type of puzzle some only of the digits of an arithmetical computation, generally a long division, are given, the others being replaced by dashes, stars or other marks. It is then required to reconstruct the computation from the clues inherent in the arrangement. For example, suppose we are given:

$$
\begin{array}{r}
2 \text{—} \text{—}) \text{—} \text{—} \ 6 \ \text{—} \text{—} (\text{—} \text{—} \text{—} \\
2 \ \text{—} \text{—} \\
\hline
\text{—} \text{—} \ 2 \ 7 \\
\text{—} \ 1 \ \ 0 \ \text{—} \\
\hline
1 \ \text{—} \text{—} \ 8 \\
\text{—} \text{—} \text{—} \ 0 \\
\hline
4 \ \text{—}
\end{array}
$$

We are then required to reconstruct the entire division from the inner clues of the computation.

Typical analysis

In this problem, the leading digit of the quotient is clearly 1. (It is recommended that the reader follow the reasoning on a separate piece of paper.) Also, the last figure of the second line must be 4. That makes the units of the divisor also 4. Hence the last digit of the quotient must be 5, to give the 0 on multiplying. The other figure of the remainder is clearly 8. The leading digit of the last product must be 1, since it cannot be 0. The second digit of the fifth line is either 1 or 2. The second digit of the sixth line is 0, 1 or 2. The middle digit of the divisor is 2, 3, 4 or 5. Therefore the first digit of the fourth line is 1 or 2, and the first digit of the third line is also 1 or 2. Quite obviously, the second digit of the third line must be 2. The last two digits of the dividend are 78. The middle digit of the divisor cannot be 5, for then the last product would be 1270, making the remainder 48 impossible. Now, since the divisor ends in 4, the units digit of the fourth line must be even. Thus the number below it must be odd. Then the middle digit of the divisor cannot be even, to make the third digit of the last product odd. Consequently it must be 3. So the last product must be 1170. The line above that must be 1218. Hence the units of the fourth line must be 6. So the second digit of the quotient must be 4 or 9. Since 4 times the divisor gives a three-digit number, this digit must be 9. This determines the whole computation at once, which results from the division 234)45678.

We shall content ourselves with but one more example, a somewhat harder one. Suppose we have given:

$$
\begin{array}{r}
---) - 2 -- 6 - (8 -- \\
-- 2 - \\
\hline
- 4 - \\
-- 3 \\
\hline
--- 1 \\
3 --- \\
\hline
- 0 -
\end{array}
$$

As before, we suggest the reader follow the reasoning on a separate piece of paper. It should be emphasized that on actually working a problem of this kind very little of the reasoning is written down, the bits of deduction being noted by entering, tentatively, small figures below their respective dashes, or crossing out one or more of them till a single figure is left as the only one tenable. What appears lengthy and perhaps formidable when written out, is quite simple when explained verbally, and takes but a fraction of the time. However, let us view this problem. Clearly, the last digit of the dividend must be 1, and the last digit of the third line 6. Hence the third digit of the fifth line must be 3, and the digit directly under it 2 or 3. As we have seen with Letter Divisions, the leading digit of the divisor is not less than the leading digit of any partial product with more digits. Hence the first digit of the divisor here is at least 3. So the leading digit of the fourth line is at least 3. But it is at most 6, since the digit under it is at least 3. Therefore the first digit of the divisor is at most 6. Since the units digit of the second product is odd, both the units digit of the divisor and the second digit of the quotient are odd. Obviously, the second digit of the quotient cannot be more than 3. Then it must be 1 or 3, whence the units of the divisor must be 3 or 1. Now if the second digit of the quotient is 3, the first digit of the divisor cannot be other than 3, to yield a three-digit product. Moreover, the first digit of the second product would have to be 9. That is impossible, since the remainder under it must be at least 3. So we cannot have 3 for the middle digit of the quotient. Thus that digit must be 1, and the units of the divisor must be 3. This requires the units of the first product to be 4, and the number above it 8. Since the third digit of the first product, by 8, is 2, and 2 is carried from the multiplication on the right, the middle digit of the divisor must be 0 or 5. It is obvious that for all possibilities the second digit of the first product must be even. Accordingly it must be 2. Now to get the product by 8, −224, if the middle digit of the divisor is 0, the whole divisor must be 403; if the middle digit is 5, the whole divisor must be 653. But if we try the latter number for the fourth row we find it impossible, since the first digit of the line above cannot be more than 9. Therefore the divisor must be 403 and the fourth line also 403. Consequently the first digit of the first product is 3, and the digit right above is also 3. The last digit of the quotient is clearly 8 or 9. If it is 9, the last product is 3627. But 4 appears right above the 6 in this. Further, the digit above the 3 would then be 4. Added to the one above that, it would require 8 next above, giving an impossible addition. Thus the last digit of the quotient cannot be 9, and so must be 8. Hence the last product is 3224 and the remainder 207. That of course determines the whole division, which must be the result of 403) 329861.

Many interesting problems of this type have been constructed, some quite difficult. As pointed out in the case of Letter Divisions, where the problem is difficult we may subdivide it into a number of special cases by trying out all possible values for an important digit and considering each case as a problem by itself. Problems of mixed or irregular type have been created, some being both fascinating and difficult. These can often be analysed by special devices.

In problems of this type it is most gratifying to find *the* answer, rather than *an* answer. By that we mean it is better to examine all possibilities, making the analysis exhaustive, so that we know when we have finished that there is no other answer, or, if such be the case, we find it. Incidentally, the examples we have given illustrate the idea.

Exercises

1. $7 - -)\, 8\, - - - - (- - $
    $\quad\quad - - \ 3$
    $\quad\quad \overline{}$
    $\quad\quad \overline{- - - - -}$
    $\quad\quad - - \ 6 \ - -$
    $\quad\quad \overline{}$

2. $7 - -) - - - - \ 4 \ -(- - - -$
    $\quad\quad - - \ 3$
    $\quad\quad \overline{}$
    $\quad\quad \overline{- - - - -}$
    $\quad\quad - - - - \ 7$
    $\quad\quad \overline{}$

3. There are two solutions.

    $- 7 -) - 1 \ - - - - - (- - - $
    $\quad\quad 3 \ - - -$
    $\quad\quad \overline{}$
    $\quad\quad \overline{- - - -}$
    $\quad\quad - 7 - -$
    $\quad\quad \overline{}$
    $\quad\quad 1 \ - - \ 3$
    $\quad\quad 1 \ - - \ 3$
    $\quad\quad \overline{}$

4.   — — 5 — —) — — 7 — — — — — —(— 6 - -
                — — — — — 7
                ——————————————————————
                — — — — — — —
                — — — — —
                ——————————————————————
                — — — — —
                — — 4 — —
                ——————————————————————

5. 6 — —) — — — — 1 (— —   **6.** 7 — —) — 0 — — — —(— 6 —
     — — 7   — — 5 —
     ——————————   ————————————
     — — — —   — — — —
     — — 6 —   — — — —
     ——————————   ————————————
                                           — — 6
                                           — — 6
                                           ————————

7. In this all the 1's are given:
                — 1 —) — — 1 — — —(— — —
                1 — — —
                ——————————————————
                1 1 — —
                — — 1
                ——————————————————
                — — — —
                — — 1 —
                ——————————————————
                1 1

8.   2 — — —) — 6 — — — 7 (— — —
                — — — —
                ——————————————————
                — — — —
                — — 1 —
                ——————————————————
                — — — —
                — — — —
                ——————————————————

9. A Square Root:

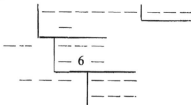

10.
```
        – 2 – ) – – 6 – 0  3 ( – – –
              1 – – –
              ‾‾‾‾‾‾‾
              4 – – –
             – 6 – –
              ‾‾‾‾‾‾‾
              – 1 – –
              – – – –
              ‾‾‾‾‾‾‾
              4 – 4
```

11. There are no other 4's:
```
        – 4 – ) – ‾ – – – – ( – – –
              – – 4
              ‾‾‾‾‾
              – – – –
              – – 4
              ‾‾‾‾‾
              4 – –
              4 – –
              ‾‾‾‾‾
```

12. Another Square Root:

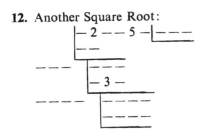

13.
```
        – 3 – ) – 1 – – – – ( – 4 –
              – – – 7
              ‾‾‾‾‾‾‾
              – – – –
              – – – –
              ‾‾‾‾‾‾‾
              – – –
              – 7 –
              ‾‾‾‾‾
```

14.
```
        – 5 – ) – – – – – – ( – – 9
              4 – 7 –
              ‾‾‾‾‾‾‾
              3 – – –
             – 6 – 2
              ‾‾‾‾‾‾‾
              – – – 0
              – – – –
              ‾‾‾‾‾‾‾
              4 7 –
```

15.
```
        – 1 – – ) – – 9 – – – – ( – – 7 –
              – – – –
              ‾‾‾‾‾‾‾
              – 5 – – –
              1 – – – –
              ‾‾‾‾‾‾‾
              – 0 – – –
              – – – 7 –
              ‾‾‾‾‾‾‾
              1 – – – –
              – – – – 2
              ‾‾‾‾‾‾‾
```

16.

$$- 6 --) 4 -- 2 - 4 -- (- 2 --$$
$$- 9 ---$$
$$\overline{}$$
$$----- $$
$$-- 2 --$$
$$\overline{}$$
$$-- 3 --$$
$$- 1 -- 4$$
$$\overline{}$$
$$----- $$
$$3 ----$$
$$\overline{}$$
$$-- 0\ 9$$

17.

$$-- 5 -) ------ 0 - (---$$
$$-- 4 -$$
$$\overline{}$$
$$--- 7 -$$
$$- 0 ---$$
$$\overline{}$$
$$----- $$
$$--- 6 -$$
$$\overline{}$$
$$-- 1$$

18. In this the sum of the divisor and quotient is odd:

$$2 ---) - 0 ----- (---$$
$$----- $$
$$\overline{}$$
$$- 0 ---$$
$$-- 1 -$$
$$\overline{}$$
$$---- 9$$
$$- 1 ---$$
$$\overline{}$$
$$4 -$$

19. In this there are no other 5's. There are four answers.

$$- 5 -) --- 5\ 5 (-- 5$$
$$- 5 -$$
$$\overline{}$$
$$--- 5$$
$$---- $$
$$\overline{}$$
$$--- 5$$
$$---- $$
$$\overline{}$$
$$5\ 5$$

20. In this there are no other 5's:

$$- 5 -) 5 -- 5 -- (---$$
$$---- $$
$$\overline{}$$
$$---- $$
$$5 ---$$
$$\overline{}$$
$$---- $$
$$---- $$

21. Six 6's! There are no more. This yields three answers.

$$- 6 -) ------ (-- 6$$
$$-- 6 -$$
$$\overline{}$$
$$-- 6 -$$
$$---- $$
$$\overline{}$$
$$- 6 --$$
$$- 6 --$$

22. Seven 7's! There are no others. There are three answers.

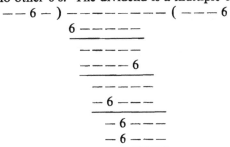

23. There are no other 6's. The dividend is a multiple of 3.

24.

VI   MAGIC NUMBER ARRANGEMENTS

Magic squares

These have been known for many centuries. By now the usual properties of such figures have become somewhat hackneyed. We shall content ourselves with an analysis of 3- and 4-squares, before passing on to other arrangements.

3-squares

There is, essentially, only one regular Magic 3-Square. Here the sum of every three numbers in a line, vertically, horizontally or diagonally, is

8	1	6
3	5	7
4	9	2

the same; 15. However, if we do not require the nine numbers to consist of as many consecutive integers, the problem becomes a bit more general. Certain properties of any such square are clear:

1. If we add the same number to (or subtract it from) each element, the result is also a magic square, with each line sum increased (or decreased) by three times the number added.

2. If we multiply (or divide) each element by the same number the result is also a magic square, with the line sum multiplied (or divided) by that number.

3. If we superimpose two (or more) magic squares, the result is also a magic square, with the line sum equal to the sum of the other two.

As will be noted, corresponding properties hold good for magic squares of any order, and also for most of the magic figures we shall consider.

Let us inquire into the essential inner relations of the elements of a 3-square. We know that the middle column gives a line sum. We enter an X for each of the numbers in this column. We know that each of the two diagonals also gives a line sum. We place an X in each of the cells of these diagonals. The figure then looks like the one adjoining, where the three X's in the middle imply that that number is counted

X	X	X
	xxx	
X	X	X

three times. These nine numbers total three line sums. But we note that the six numbers in the top and bottom rows by themselves account for two line sums. Hence, since all the numbers together give three line sums, the middle number taken three times must account for a line sum. That is, the central number must be one-third of a line sum. For whole numbers, then, the line sum must be divisible by 3. It cannot, for example, be such a number as 50. Also, the sum of all the nine numbers must be 9 times the central number.

70

It follows now that each of the four pairs of numbers in alignment with the central number must have a sum double the central number; which sum, incidentally, must be an even number. It may also be observed that the difference between any consecutive pair of corner numbers must be less than the middle number. It is also obvious that no number can be twice as large as the middle number.

Again starting with the blank figure, suppose we consider the four numbers marked with X and Y. If the upper left hand corner number be added to the two X numbers we get a line sum. If it be added to the two Y numbers we also get a line sum. Thus adding twice this corner number to the sum of the other four numbers gives two line sums. But adding the two numbers in the cells with dots also gives two line sums. So twice the number in the upper left hand corner is equal to the sum of the two numbers in the cells with dots. A similar fact is true for each of the corner numbers. It is to be noted that the sum of each pair of dotted numbers must then be even. It follows then that the four numbers in the middles of the sides are either all odd or all even.

X	Y	·
X	·	Y

Again, let us try to build up a magic 3-square. Suppose we place three 1's so that we have a 1 in each row and a 1 in each column. That is easily done, but we desire a 1 in each of the diagonals also. We observe that we cannot get both diagonals covered. The best we can do is shown by the figure to the left. Here the second-

1		
		1
	1	

ary diagonal is left blank. However, we can get round that difficulty by putting $\frac{1}{2}$ in each cell of this diagonal. The line sum is then $1\frac{1}{2}$. To avoid fractions, we double each figure, obtaining the array alongside. It will be seen now that this array is fundamental. We

1		$\frac{1}{2}$
	$\frac{1}{2}$	1
$\frac{1}{2}$	1	

2		1
	1	2
1	2	

can form any 3-square by superimposing a number of such figures. In particular, if we superimpose on each other two of the second type after one is turned about 180°, we get a square containing a 1 in each cell. We can keep subtracting arrays of the type here discussed from the standard 3-square to obtain a square containing only blanks.

Suppose now we consider a specific problem regarding the 3-square. We undertake to form one with nine different primes having a minimum sum.

Before proceeding to this we may describe a convenient method the writer has often employed. It is apparent the prime number 2 cannot be used in this connection, as also in many similar problems. Since all the other primes are odd, we add 1 to each and then divide by 2, getting a sequence of smaller numbers to handle. These are, 1, 2, 3, 4, 6, 7, 9, 10, 12, 15, 16, 19, 21, 22, 24, 27, 30, 31, 34, 36, 37, 40, 42, 45, 49, 51, 52, 54, 55, etc. We may now play with these, conveniently using the numbered blocks of a game of lotto.

For our problem, we then focus attention on the central number. We recall that the other eight numbers must consist of four pairs each having a sum double the central number. We consider 6 for the central number. Then we must have four pairs totalling 12. But there are only two such pairs. The same holds good for 7. For 9 we get three pairs, for 10 two, for 12, 15, 16, each three. However, for 19, we get five pairs:

16	
19	31
1	22

22, 16; 31, 7; 34, 4; 36, 2; 37, 1. Again, we see which, if any, number can serve as a corner number. Twice such a number must be the sum of two others. We start with 16. Only one other pair gives a total 32, 31 and 1. Hence we have the array on the right. We next enter the two numbers opposite 31 and 1, namely

16	37	4
7	19	31
34	1	22

7 and 37. That then leaves two corner numbers to be filled in. Since a line sum is here 57, we find the upper right corner must be 4. Now 4 happens to be one of the permissible numbers in our five selected pairs. From the nature of our analysis this must fit, and we have the

31	73	7
13	37	61
67	1	43

solution shown. We now test the remaining numbers of our five sets for perhaps another solution with the same minimal sum. But there are no other possibilities. Replacing the numbers we have found by their corresponding primes, we get the solution shown just above.

4-squares

Let us now form a somewhat similar analysis of 4-squares. For convenience,

1	2	3	4
5	6	7	8
9	10	11	12
13	14	15	16

we shall number the cells as in the accompanying figure. Suppose that in any magic square we take the total of all the numbers marked with an X. These twelve numbers consist of two horizontal line sums and the four inner numbers. But they also consist of two vertical line sums and the four corner numbers. It follows then, since all line sums are equal, that the four corner numbers have the same total as the four inner numbers. Again, we mark the eight numbers of the two diagonals. These total two line sums. But they consist of the four inner numbers and the four corner numbers. As we have

X	X	X	X
	x	x	
	x	x	
x	x	x	x

seen, these two tetrads of numbers have equal sums. Since the total of all eight numbers is two line sums, each tetrad represents a line sum. That is, the four inner numbers total a line sum, and the four corner numbers total a line sum. Further, the four numbers here marked with X's must total a line sum, since, if we add the four inner numbers to them, a total of one line sum by themselves, we get two line sums. Similarly, the numbers in Cells 5, 8, 9, 12 have a line sum for total. Again, the two end numbers of the second row have the same sum as the two inner numbers of the third row; since we get a line sum by adding the two inner numbers of the second row to either pair. Similarly, the pair in Cells 6 and 7 have the same sum as those in Cells 9 and 12; those in Cells 2 and 14 the same sum as those in 7 and 11; those in 3 and 15 the same sum as those in 6 and 10. Once more, the pair of end numbers of the first row have the same sum as the pair of middle numbers of the last row; since we get a line sum by adding to either pair the two middle numbers of the first row. Similarly, the sum of the numbers in Cells 2 and 3 is the same as that of the numbers in Cells 13 and 16; the sum of those in Cells 5 and 9 the same as those in 4 and 16; that of the numbers in 1 and 13 the same as that of those in Cells 8 and 12. Finally, we note that the two numbers marked X here have the same sum as those marked with a dash; since if we add to either pair the other two corner numbers we get a line sum. Similarly, the sum of the numbers in Cells 1 and 16 is the same as that of those in Cells 7 and 10.

An application

Let us apply our knowledge: suppose we are given the incomplete magic square adjoining. We are asked to complete it. We know that the sum of the numbers in Cells 13 and 16—that is, 11—must be the same as that of the numbers in Cells 2 and 3. Hence the number in Cell 3 must be 5. Cells 1 and 16 have the sum 32. That must be the same as the sum of the numbers in Cells 7 and 10. Hence we must have 13 in Cell 10. Now Cells 6 and 10 have the sum 37. That must be the same as the sum of the numbers in Cells 3 and 15. Hence we must have 32 in Cell 15. Cells 1 and 13 have the sum 41. That must be the same as the sum of the numbers in Cells 8 and 12. Hence we must have 15 in Cell 8.

73

Cells 5 and 8 have the sum 27. That must be the same as the sum of the numbers in Cells 10 and 11. Hence we must have 14 in Cell 11. Cells 6 and 7 total 43. Cells 9 and 12 must have this sum.

31	6	5	28
12	24	19	15
17	13	14	26
10	27	32	1

Hence we have 17 in Cell 9. Cells 7 and 11 total 33. Hence Cells 2 and 14 total 33. Hence Cell 14 must contain 27. Cells 6 and 11 total 38. Hence Cells 4 and 13 total 38. Hence Cell 4 must contain 28. We have then completed our Magic Square without knowing what the line sum must be! This method of analysis helps us to create problems of this type, indicates what is sufficient to solve the problem uniquely, and shows when a required arrangement is impossible.

			1
		1	
1			
		1	

Before leaving this topic, we may consider what appears to be an essential building block of a Magic 4-Square. If we place four 1's as shown

+1	−1		
−1	+1		

we observe that we have a magic square. The question arises: can we build up any magic 4-square by superimposing a proper number of such magic squares in any of the eight possible positions? The answer seems to be 'Yes', if we are permitted to include building blocks of the type shown alongside.

Multiplication magic squares

A good deal of what we have presented applies equally well to this type of figure, where the numbers in alignment are multiplied instead of added. In this case the 1's do not affect products, just as 0's do not affect additions in ordinary magic squares. Duplicating the procedure of the last paragraph with other numbers, we may thus build up any number of multiplication magic squares. Of course, where minimum products are required, we consider, besides 1, the smallest primes and their powers: 2, 4, 8, etc., 3, 9, etc., as well as 5, 7 and 11.

Magic cubes

Just as we have magic squares, we have magic cubes. We may divide a cube, for example, into 64 smaller cubicles, and place a number in each of these cubicles with the requirement that every four numbers in a straight line shall have the same sum. Or we may have a cubic wire arrangement where a number is attached to every crossing, with the same requirement. In the former illustration, we may imagine a number of beads occupying each cubicle.

We shall content ourselves with giving an illustration of a seven-cube constructed with consecutive integers:

I

322	87	153	261	33	141	207
29	144	210	318	90	149	264
86	152	260	32	147	206	321
143	209	317	89	148	263	35
151	266	31	146	205	320	85
208	316	88	154	262	34	142
265	30	145	204	319	91	150

II

100	215	323	95	161	269	41
157	272	37	103	211	326	98
214	329	94	160	268	40	99
271	36	102	217	325	97	156
328	93	159	267	39	105	213
42	101	216	324	96	155	270
92	158	273	38	104	212	327

III

277	49	108	223	331	54	162
334	50	165	280	45	111	219
48	107	222	330	53	168	276
56	164	279	44	110	218	333
106	221	336	52	167	275	47
163	278	43	109	224	332	55
220	335	51	166	274	46	112

IV

62	170	285	1	116	231	339
119	227	342	58	173	281	4
169	284	7	115	230	338	61
226	341	57	172	287	3	118
283	6	114	229	337	60	175
340	63	171	286	2	117	225
5	113	228	343	59	174	282

V

232	298	70	178	293	9	124
289	12	120	235	301	66	181
297	69	177	292	8	123	238
11	126	234	300	65	180	288
68	176	291	14	122	237	296
125	233	299	64	179	294	10
182	290	13	121	236	295	67

VI

17	132	240	306	71	186	252
74	189	248	20	128	243	302
131	239	305	77	185	251	16
188	247	19	127	242	308	73
245	304	76	184	250	15	130
246	18	133	241	307	72	187
303	75	183	249	21	129	244

VII

194	253	25	140	199	314	79
202	310	82	190	256	28	136
259	24	139	198	313	78	193
309	81	196	255	27	135	201
23	138	197	312	84	192	258
80	195	254	26	134	200	315
137	203	311	83	191	257	22

Imagine these placed together in the order given so as to form a cube of 343 cells. Every plate parallel to a given face forms a magic square. There are 21 of these. Besides, the rectangular array common to a plane through each pair of opposite edges gives a magic square, thus yielding a total of 27 magic squares. Further, every seven numbers in a line parallel to an edge gives the same line total. There are 49×3 of these. There are, besides, 21×2 diagonals parallel to the faces of the cube. There are four 'solid diagonals', giving a total of 193 alignments with the characteristic sum 1204.

The mnemonic for the construction of this will be clear from the following: As is usual with magic squares, we consider the first column to follow the last column cyclically, and the first row to follow the last in similar fashion. (We might visualize something like a torus, cut and flattened out.) In the same manner we visualize the first plate as succeeding the last. With this convention in mind, following the 1 on Plate IV, the first seven numbers are entered in cyclic order. Then we jump two spaces to the right on the next block to begin entering the next seven numbers on that in the same manner. This is continued till seven sets of seven numbers are placed. The next 49 numbers are placed in like manner, beginning just below the last of the previous set. This is continued till all numbers are placed.

Other magic arrays

Once we remove the restriction to the magic square form, a whole vista of novel and entertaining possibilities opens up. Some are easy to handle, some are not quite so easy, some rather hard, some exceedingly difficult—but all are interesting. We shall analyse some of the simpler forms, leaving it to the exercises which follow to show the possibilities of this type of recreation.

It may be stressed that the kind of analysis we apply to the more simple forms, apparently not altogether necessary to effect our purpose, is typical of the kind that is often effective in the more complicated cases.

Let us start with a very simple problem, not too much different from a magic square. Suppose we are required to distribute the numbers from

1 to 9, one in each circle, so that every four forming a square shall have

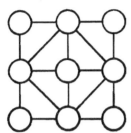

the same sum. Presumably just a few trials will yield a solution. However, let us see how it reacts to analysis. We have six squares. Suppose we place an X for every number of each of the four smaller squares. Then we have an array that looks like the one just below. This represents four square sums. Now the four corner numbers total a square sum. If crossed out, we have three square sums left. The sum of the four side numbers is a square sum. So if we cross out every double X on the sides we remove two

square sums, leaving only one square sum. But we have left four middle numbers. Hence four times the middle number is a square sum. Further, the eight outer numbers constitute two square sums. Hence the sum of all the numbers must be 9 times the middle number.

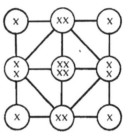

Again, suppose we place an X for each of the numbers in the small squares at the upper right and lower left. These eight numbers are then two

square sums. If we remove the four side numbers we have a square sum

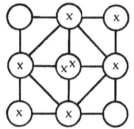

left. This consists of twice the middle number, and two opposite corner numbers. The two opposite corner numbers then total half a square sum. So far, the discussion has been general. In our specific problem the sum of all the numbers is 45; hence the central number must be 5 and the sum of each pair of opposite corner numbers 10. We now take an extreme number, 9, and see where it can be placed. We find that if it has a

side position two pairs of numbers excluding a 5 must total 6. That cannot be. So we place 9 at a corner and 1 at the opposite corner. Now 9 and 5 are 14. Hence the two side numbers adjoining the 9 must total 6. They must then be 2 and 4. The array is then readily completed.

In the following figure, suppose we are asked to distribute the numbers from 1 to 13, one number in each circle, so that every four forming a square shall have the same sum. There are ten squares here.

For convenience, we letter the numbers according to their positions, and represent the square sum by s. Further, we shall let A represent the sum of all the A numbers, B the sum of all the B numbers, etc. Clearly,

$$A + B + C + X = 91.$$

Again, since the A numbers by themselves constitute a square, and the B numbers also,

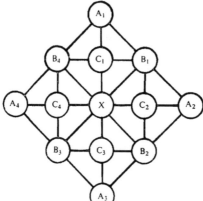

$$A = B = s.$$

Hence

$$C + X = 91 - 2s.$$

From the discussion of the previous problem, $s = 4X$ and $A + B = 8X$. Also $B + C = 8X$. Hence $A = C$, whence $A = B = C = 4X$, and $13X = 91$. Hence $X = 7$. Also, $A_1 + A_3 = A_2 + A_4 = B_1 + B_3 = B_2 + B_4 = 14$. If we now choose all the A's odd and also C_1 and C_3, a solution appears at once (From here on we shall dispense with the circles at the vertices). Three observations are in order here:

1. Where we have a symmetric array, with a centre and an odd number of numbers, it is often conducive to a rapid solution to place the mean of the numbers in the centre and complementary pairs total-ling double that mean at opposite positions in the figure. In such a case we pay attention to only half of the figure, say the upper half in the last problem, knowing that if the array fits here it will automatically fit below. A similar procedure may be followed with an even num-ber of numbers without a central position. Of course, that may not work with more restrictive problems. In fact, in some a symmetric solution

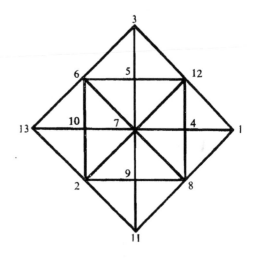

may be found impossible, though a solution of irregular type may still exist.

2. Where difficulty is encountered, it often helps to find a consistent distribution of the odd numbers before placing them in any specific positions.

3. Where we have consecutive integers, it must be realized that another solution is obtained (in exceptional cases that is the old one turned about)

by replacing each number by its complement. At times it may be shown that one of the extreme numbers has, say, a certain position. If the number of numbers is even, we may at our pleasure take either extreme in such a position. Again, where we have a number of cases to examine, we may learn that half are obtained from the other by using complementary values. We may then conveniently restrict ourselves to one set of values rather than two.

Let us now consider the last figure from a different standpoint. Suppose, instead of equal square sums, we require

a) that the sum of every three numbers connected in alignment shall be the same;

b) that each set of five in alignment shall have the same sum.

We note that there are ten triads in alignment and two pentads. Let the first sum be t, the second p.

Again,

$$A + B + C + X = 91.$$

Clearly,

$$A + B + X = 3t, \quad B + C + X = 3t,$$

whence $A = C$. Also,

$$A + C + 2X = 2p. \quad \therefore \ C + X = p.$$

$$\therefore \ A_1 + A_3 = C_2 + C_4 \ \text{and} \ A_2 + A_4 = C_1 + C_3.$$

From the first two equations above,

$$C = 91 - 3t.$$

Hence

$$X = p + 3t - 91.$$

Also,

$$A = 91 - 3t.$$

From these, $B = 3t - p$.

Again, $B + C_1 + C_3 = 2t$. Hence

$$C_1 + C_3 = C_2 + C_4 = A_1 + A_3 = A_2 + A_4.$$

Hence A and C are even. Hence t is odd. Further,

$$A + B_1 + B_3 = 2t. \quad \text{Hence} \quad B_1 + B_3 = B_2 + B_4.$$

Hence B is even. Hence X is odd and p is odd. Also,

$$p = A_1 + A_3 + C_1 + C_3 + X$$
$$= A_1 + A_3 + (2t - B) + X,$$
$$A_1 + A_3 = p - 2t + 3t - p - p - 3t + 91$$
$$= 91 - p - 2t.$$

Hence $A_1 + A_3$ is even. Further,

$$A_2 + A_4 = 91 - 2t - p, \ \text{etc.}$$

79

At this point it readily occurs to us to use complementary values. Taking for X the mean value 7, for t three times this mean value, or 21, and for p

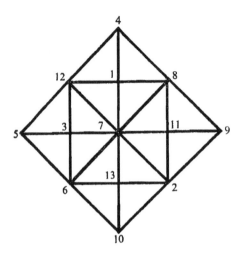

five times this mean, or 35, the complementary pairs must total 14. Having done this, the pentads are automatically provided for. Further, as we have seen, if we arrange the numbers properly in the upper half of the figure, the rest will be taken care of automatically. Again, we try placing all the odd numbers. Suppose we array them along the horizontal diagonal and at the points C_1 and C_3. Let us take the extreme numbers, 1 and 13, at the last two points and the other odd numbers in the order 5, 3, 7, 11, 9. We have to select two even numbers totalling 16, for A_1 and B_4. Let us choose 4 and 12. Here the 4 for B_4 will not fit the horizontal triad with 1. However, if we place the 12 there, and the 4 at A_1, we automatically complete the figure as shown.

Of course, this array lends itself readily to this kind of complementary arrangement. There are other arrays, however, equally plausible, where a complementary setting is either impossible or extremely difficult to find. Such require more detailed analysis, and even then a good deal of trial work.

Cross-pentagons

We now discuss a different type of array. To simplify our figure in appearance, suppose we have ten numbers distributed, one at each vertex or crossing, so that every four in a straight line shall have the same sum. If the array at the right represents a solution, we observe also that the first one on the next page is an equivalent solution, where the same sets of four numbers occur in each

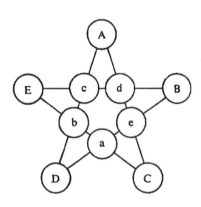

case. This is an instance where, if we are given a set of numbers to arrange, we may place an extreme number, say the largest, wherever we please, and go on from there. We also observe an unsymmetric equivalent

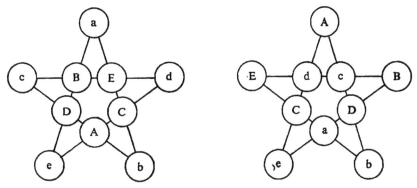

rearrangement in the second figure above. Thus a single solution gives rise in this way to a variety of others. Further, each gives another solution if each number is replaced by its difference from another that is at least 1 more than the largest of the ten numbers. We note also that we get a similar magic pentagon if we multiply each number of the array by the same number, or if we superimpose two such figures and add corresponding numbers. Various interesting puzzles may be solved conveniently by judiciously applying these simple ideas.

We may note also that each of the following changes, each equivalent to the superimposition of a simple magic cross pentagon, increases each line sum by 2:

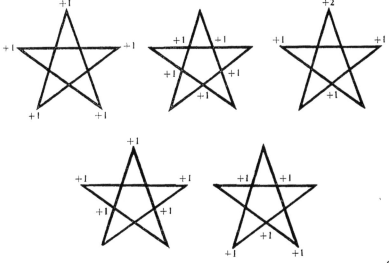

The following types of change do not affect the characteristic total:

These may be combined in a number of ways. For example, the following types of change do not affect the line totals:

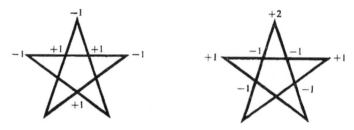

By means of these changes every magic pentagon can be reduced to one with 1's only, or 0's only, at the intersections. Conversely, every magic pentagon can be built up by starting with 1's.

Suppose now we consider finding a solution to the cross-pentagon array. We have:

$$B + E + d + c = s,$$
$$B + D + a + e = s,$$
$$E + C + b + a = s,$$
$$A + D + b + c = s,$$
$$A + C + d + e = s.$$

Subtracting the sum of the last two equations from the sum of the first three, we have, on dividing by 2,

$$a + B + E - A = \frac{s}{2}.$$

From the transposed figure, we get similarly,

$$A + c + d - a = \frac{s}{2}.$$

This makes s necessarily an even number.

Let us suppose we are required to use the consecutive integers from 1 to 10. The sum of all the numbers is 55. Clearly, the five tetrad sums use each number twice. Hence $5s = 110$ and s is 22. Here $s/2$ is 11, an *odd* number. As already observed, we may take any particular vertex as an odd number. We have 5 odd and 5 even numbers to work with. Placing an odd number at A, only three arrays of the odd numbers are possible:

Here the positions of the odd numbers are marked by heavy dots. Now we have seen that the second form is rigidly transformable to the first. Further, by complements, the third is transformable to the second; the odd numbers in the new position taking the place of the even numbers. Hence we may assume the first form as typical.

At this point a few trials will exhaust all apparently tenable arrangements and we deduce the problem impossible. We must then look for other types of solution.

Before proceeding, we may show another device for reducing the size of the numbers. If, in the standard case, we add 1 to each outer number, all the numbers are then even (and duplicated) and the line sum is increased by 2 to 24. If we now divide each number by 2, the line sum becomes 12. We have then the numbers 1 to 5 in the outer positions, and 1 to 5 in the inner positions. Of course, here the magnitude of the numbers does not matter much. On the other hand, we might now continue our analysis with the new sets of numbers, even separating these into odd and even categories. Such procedure can, and often does, yield results.

We ask then, is a solution in non-consecutive integers possible? We readily see that it is, and seek a solution with minimum line sum or with minimum largest number. Since $5s$ must in any case be twice the sum of all the numbers, the sum of the numbers must be divisible by 5. We shall not devote space to a detailed discussion of the solution, but will merely state that there are several solutions with minimal sum of all the numbers 60. Among these, the minimum largest number used is 12.

Carrying out a somewhat more elaborate, but similar, analysis for prime numbers, we find a solution with minimal sum of all the primes. Here the line sum is 72.

The solutions of this, and the problem discussed above, are left to the reader.

83

Cross-hexagons

In the adjoining figures, let us suppose, first, that we are to array the numbers from 1 to 12 so that the sum of every four in alignment shall be the same.

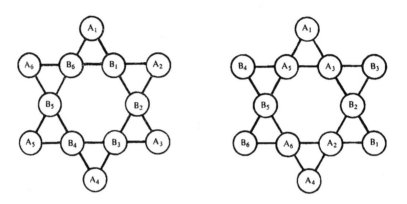

Before proceeding to any analysis at all we note that for any solution represented by the first figure the second figure is also a solution.

The sum of all the numbers is 78. If we take all the six tetrads we note that every number occurs twice, so that, if t be the tetrad sum;

$$2A + 2B = 6t, \text{ whence } A + B = 3t.$$

But $A + B = 78$. Hence t must be 26.

Again, from the three tetrads forming the triangle $A_1 A_3 A_5$,

$$2(A_1 + A_3 + A_5) + B = 3t = 78.$$

Hence $A_1 + A_3 + A_5 = A_2 + A_4 + A_6$. Hence A and B are even. Suppose now we try to obtain a solution by placing complementary pairs of numbers totalling 13 in symmetric positions. Then

$$A_1 + A_4 = A_2 + A_5 = A_3 + A_6 = 13.$$

Thus the sum of all the A's is 39, an *odd* number. So in any case a solution

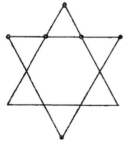

by complementary pairs is impossible. Let us then seek to place the six odd numbers. Can we have them at the six outer vertices? In that case, $A = 36$, and $A_1 + A_3 + A_5 = A_2 + A_4 + A_6 = 18$. But no three odd numbers can have this sum. So we try a different array. Suppose we place the odd numbers in the positions indicated by the heavy dots. We choose a set of four odd numbers totalling 26, and place the other two at the top and bottom vertices. We try 5, 11, 9, 1 and get a solution very readily: Another solution is:

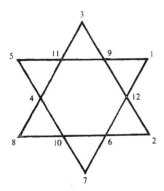 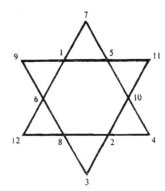

Of course, we can transform either solution as indicated above. Again, we get other solutions by replacing each number by its difference from 13.

Here the conditions are so loose that we have considerable freedom of choice. This enables us to impose additional conditions purely for convenience. However, where the conditions are more stringent, or where the possibilities are multifarious, this may not be done at all freely. In fact, in some difficult arrays, a solution following a regular pattern is often impossible. On the other hand, *where there is a solution*, a stringency of conditions often drives us to it.

Let us now take another problem about the same figure: Suppose we require the six triads of numbers forming the small outer triangles to have the same sum. Taking the sum of the nine numbers forming the triangles having the apices A_1, A_3, A_5,

$$A_1 + A_3 + A_5 + B = A_2 + A_4 + A_6 + B = 3t,$$

where t is a triangular sum. Hence

$$A_1 + A_3 + A_5 = A_2 + A_4 + A_6$$

and A is even. Now $A + B = 78$. Taking the sum of all the triangular triads,

$$A + 2B = 6t.$$

Hence

$$B = 6t - 78, \qquad A = 156 - 6t.$$

Then t is at least 17 and at most 22. We now note that if we have a solution for any value of t we have another solution by replacing each member by its difference from 13. The sum of a triangular triad in the new figure

85

is then 39-t. Thus if we find a solution for $t = 17$ we have one for $t = 22$, and vice versa. So in the analysis we might make, we restrict ourselves conveniently to the possible values 17, 18 or 19 for t, since these are equivalent to 22, 21, 20 respectively. Suppose we try $t = 19$, making $A = 42$ and $B = 36$. Again we try a distribution of the odd numbers, as shown on the left. We readily find a solution, as shown below.

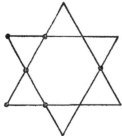

Now we note two other completed triangles in the figure, $A_1 A_3 A_5$ and $A_2 A_4 A_6$. Suppose we require these also to have the sum t. Then $A = 2t$. Since $A = 156 - 6t$, $8t = 156$, making t a fraction. Hence it is impossible to have all the eight triangles with the same sum in consecutive integers. We seek then a solution of this problem in non-consecutive integers, and may require also that the sum of all the numbers used, or, instead, the largest number used, or the triangular sum, t, be a minimum.

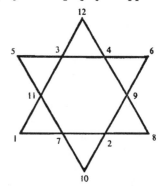

Obviously, $A = 2t$. Let the total sum of all the twelve numbers be a. Hence $A + B = a$. As before, $A + 2B = 6t$, whence $B = 6t - a$, $A = 2a - 6t$. Further, since $A = 2t$, $a = 4t$. We also note:

$$B_1 + B_6 = A_3 + A_5, \quad B_2 + B_3 = A_1 + A_5, \quad B_4 + B_5 = A_1 + A_3.$$

Adding the last three;

$$B = 2(A_1 + A_3 + A_5) = 2(A_2 + A_4 + A_6) = A.$$

Hence $A = B = 2t$. Also,

$$B_1 + B_6 = A_3 + A_5 \text{ and } A_2 + A_6 = B_3 + B_4.$$

Adding,

$$A_2 + A_6 + B_1 + B_6 = A_3 + A_5 + B_3 + B_4.$$

Also,

$$A_6 + A_2 = B_4 + B_3 \text{ and } A_5 + A_3 = B_6 + B_1.$$

Adding,

$$A_2 + A_3 + A_5 + A_6 = B_1 + B_3 + B_4 + B_6,$$

whence

$$A - (A_1 + A_4) = B - (B_2 + B_5).$$

Since $A = B$,

$$A_1 + A_4 = B_2 + B_5.$$

Now we have shown that three pairs of linear tetrads must be equal. We now modify our problem by requiring that in addition to the eight equal triangular sums we have all six linear tetrads with equal sums. If each of the latter be s, then

$$3s = 2(A_1 + A_3 + A_5) + B = A + B = 4t.$$

Hence s is a multiple of 4 and t a multiple of 3. If we take $t = 3p$, $s = 4p$, $A = B = 6p$, $a = 12t$. Further,

$$A_1 + A_4 + B_2 + B_5 = a - 2s = 4p.$$
$$\therefore \quad A_1 + A_4 = B_2 + B_5 = 2p.$$

It now follows that the entire array consists necessarily of six complementary pairs. Further, in any case, the sum of all the numbers used must be a multiple of 12. In this case the smallest value for a can be 84, for $p = 7$. Here every complementary sum is 14. We can try placing the odd numbers at the outer vertices and we readily get a solution like the left one.

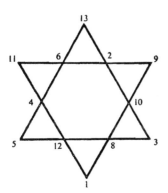

Following out a similar, though necessarily more detailed, procedure in the case of prime numbers, a minimal solution is soon found, and this is shown just below.

The type of problem we have been considering opens up many possibilities for investigation and entertainment. Many are as fascinating as they are difficult. Among the latter are a number the writer had been holding back as possible tie-breakers in contests. What intrigues the writer in this type of recreation is the fact that extended mathematical knowledge is no direct help in solving most of the puzzles that may be presented, but there is unlimited scope for personal ingenuity. Innumerable devices of a specialized type are often applied in the more difficult cases. We cannot give space for further discussion of these here.

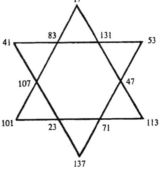

The question does arise, however, as to the possibilities of applying the more elaborate mathematical processes to the solution of this type of problem. It seems to the writer that the application of certain types of combinatory analysis may actually yield

87

the number of solutions possible without giving a single one. On the other hand, we may conceive of the application of algebraic procedure to some of the problems, in the following way:

Suppose we have n consecutive integers to distribute in such a way that the sums of certain combinations will be equal (we take a simple illustration). Now suppose r of these conditions are independent, where $r<n$. We have then $n - r$ degrees of freedom. However, conceiving of the n numbers as so many unknowns, we still do know certain things about them *a priori*. For example, the sum of the first power of all the numbers is $n(n + 1)/2$. The sum of the second power is $n(n + 1)(2n + 1)/6$; etc. We may then write down $n - r$ additional equations to the r independent equations we have presupposed. The problem then is to solve these n simultaneous equations. We could, presumably, eliminate $n - 1$ of the unknowns. But when we realize that that would yield an equation of degree $(n - r)!$ the prospect becomes prohibitive. Of course, someone may in time hit on a procedure that is both simple and effective. If such were found, this type of intellectual play would become stereotyped. However, we could always introduce new types of question not amenable to such analysis. For example, in the type of illustration presupposed, restricting the choice of numbers to primes with a minimum condition would serve as a point of departure.

We close this chapter with a number of exercises, preceded by some suggestive comments.

Comments on Exercises

2.   There are three solutions in all.

12.   It would be interesting to find all basic solutions.

18.   There are four basic solutions.

19.   The writer does not know *why* it is impossible to solve this problem, other than that he has tried all combinations exhaustively and found none would serve.

20.   Try to utilize the relations of the numbers in the basic 3-square.

It is remarkable indeed that we can complete one or three triangles under the required conditions, but not two. Can we fill four triangles with the numbers from 1 to 24? The writer has not tried. And how about using primes? This also the author has not tried.

28.   This offers a chance to apply the treatment in the text. It will be noted that the main diagonals have the same sum.

30.   It will be noted that the pair of numbers marked X have the same sum as those marked Y.

31.   Cf. comment on Ex. 28.

32. There are many solutions to this loose problem.

36. This is incapable of solution.

38. There are four solutions.

40. It may be noted in all such distributions that the sum of every pair of numbers on an edge equals that of the pair on the opposite edge, so that the difference of the numbers on a solid diagonal is the same for all four such numbers.

46. There are 24 distinct solutions.

62. There are only four solutions.

66. This is somewhat more difficult. One method of proceeding is to find consistent positions for the odd numbers.

82a, b, c. See the text, p. 83.

88. It may be shown that for any solution there is an equivalent rearrangement.

91. It is curious that, even without specifying the positions of any of the numbers, in no case can a magic three-square be included in the array.

92. There are two solutions.

93. The result here is unique. It is an interesting exercise to prove that.

101. This is rather difficult. Besides employing the analysis of the 4-square in the text, we would recommend reducing the numbers as explained before and then using lotto blocks.

102. This the author has not yet done. It is suggested that the even (or odd) numbers be placed at the heavy dots.

103. Here too the odd numbers may be placed at the heavy dots. This exercise is fairly difficult.

104. Also quite difficult.

105. So is this. It must be realized the alternating triads of outer triangular vertices must have the same sum.

106. This the author has not yet succeeded in doing. Curiously, there was no difficulty in getting the square sums equal, and in various ways, but in each case one or two of the hexad sums was one or two off.

107. This problem, the writer feels, will challenge the ingenuity of anyone. It was only after an intensive, varied and sustained attack that the author finally solved it. Curiously, any correct solution may be arranged in $6 \times 8 \times 36 \times 36 \times 36$ (i.e. 2239488) ways; also the complementary solution. It is clear that each of the six linear triads radiating from the centre has the same sum. It is suggested that the number 46 (or 1) be placed at the centre.

Exercises

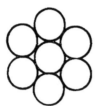

1. Distribute the numbers from 1 to 7, one in each circle, so that:
a) The sum of every three in alignment is the same;
b) the sum of either alternate set of three numbers in the outer ring is also this sum.

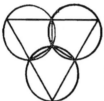

2. Arrange the numbers from 1 to 7 so that:
a) every triad on a side has the same sum;
b) every circular tetrad has the same sum;
c) both sums are equal.
Find all possible solutions.

3. Numbers 1 to 10.
a) Three linear triad sums equal.
b) Three linear tetrad sums equal.

4. Find a second solution to Ex. 3.

5. Numbers 1 to 8.
Four small triangular sums equal, and the same as the sum of the top and bottom middle numbers.

6. Find a solution of Ex. 5 in prime numbers.

7. Numbers 1 to 9.
Six equal linear triad sums.

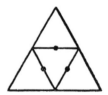

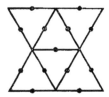

8. Numbers 1 to 21.
Every triad of numbers on the side of a small triangle has the same sum.
There are 13 such triads.

9. Numbers 1 to 14.
Every three in alignment have the same sum.

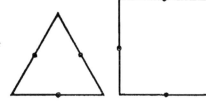

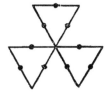

10. Numbers 1 to 16.
Every three on the side of a small triangle have the same sum.

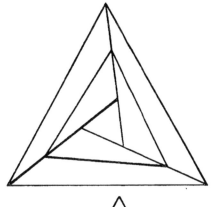

11. Numbers 1 to 9.
a) Every three forming an equilateral triangle and every three in alignment have the same sum.
b) Every four in alignment have the same sum.

12. Numbers 1 to 12.
Every tetrad in alignment has the same sum. There are six such tetrads.

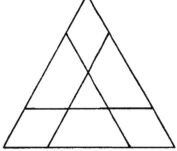

91

13. Find a second solution to Ex. 12.

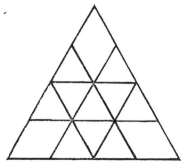

14. Numbers 1 to 15.
3 linear triads with equal sums;
3 linear tetrads with equal sums;
3 linear pentads with equal sums.

15. Find a second solution to Ex. 14.

16. Numbers 1 to 10.
3 equal tetrads in alignment;
3 equal triads in alignment;
3 equal dyads connected by lines.

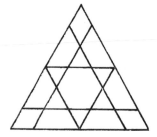

17. Numbers 1 to 21.
3 equal linear tetrad sums;
3 equal linear pentad sums;
3 equal linear hexad sums.

18. Numbers 1 to 6.
Three equal linear triad sums. Find all possible basic solutions.

19. Numbers 1 to 12.
Six equal linear triad sums.

20. Numbers 1 to 18.
Nine equal linear triad sums.
Find more than one solution.

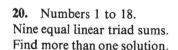

92

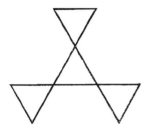

21. The Clover-Leaf. Numbers 1 to 9. Four equal triangular sums.

22. In last figure, 3 equal linear tetrad sums.
23. In Ex.21, both 4 equal triangular sums and 3 equal linear tetrad sums. (Not necessarily with consecutive integers.)
24. Solution of Ex. 23 with minimum sum of all numbers.
25. The same as Ex. 24, but using prime numbers only.

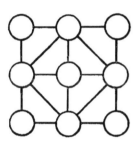

26. These represent 9 saucers containing beans. All told, there are 54 beans. There is at least 1 bean in each saucer. No two saucers contain the same number. One saucer has only 1 bean. Another has just 3 beans. Only one saucer has a number of beans of two digits. Each of the six squares of saucers contains the same number of beans. How are they distributed?

27. In the last figure place a different prime number in each dish so that every four dishes forming a square shall have the same sum, and the total of all shall be a minimum.

28. Numbers 1 to 16, one at each meeting of two lines. There are fourteen sets of four each forming a square. All the sets have the same total. How are the numbers distributed?

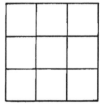

29. The 18 numbers below are to be separated into two groups of nine each so that each group may be arranged as in Ex. 26, in such a way that the six squares formed shall have the same sum within each group:

$$1 \quad 2 \quad 3 \quad 4 \quad 5 \quad 6 \quad 7 \quad 8 \quad 9$$
$$10 \quad 11 \quad 13 \quad 14 \quad 15 \quad 17 \quad 18 \quad 25 \quad 30$$

93

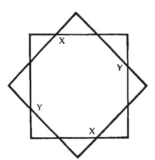

30. Numbers 1 to 16.
Eight equal linear tetrad sums.

31. Numbers 1 to 24.
18 equal square sums.

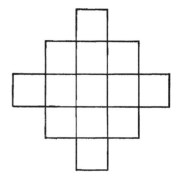

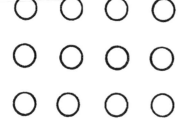

32. Omitting one number from 1 to 13, arrange the twelve so that each of the four columns shall have the same sum and each of the rows shall have the same sum.

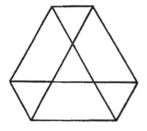

33. Numbers 1 to 9.
Seven equal triangular sums.

34. With the figure of Ex. 33, use nine different primes of minimum sum to get seven equal triangular totals.

35. Numbers 1 to 12.
3 equal linear triad sums and
3 equal linear tetrad sums.

36. Numbers 1 to 12.
6 equal linear triad sums and
3 equal linear tetrad sums.

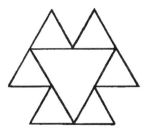

37. Numbers 1 to 12.
7 equal triangular sums.

38. Numbers 1 to 9.
6 equal linear triad sums.
Find all basic solutions.

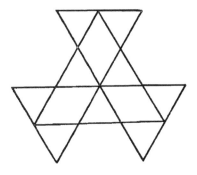

39. Numbers 1 to 16.
Three equal linear triad sums;
three equal linear tetrad sums;
three equal linear pentad sums.

95

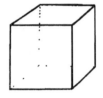

40. Numbers 1 to 8, one at each vertex of the cube. Every four on a face have the same sum.

41. In the last figure, the numbers from 1 to 12 are to be placed with one number on each edge so that every square shall have the same sum.
42. Instead of the consecutive numbers in Ex. 40, use the numbers 50, 250, 350, 500, 550, 700, 800, 1000.
43. In the last problem, do the same with the numbers 560, 700, 770, 840, 980, 1120, 1190, 1260.

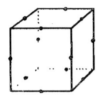

44. Numbers 1 to 20.
Every set of four forming a square shall have the same sum. There are 15 such sets.

45. Numbers 1 to 22
8 linear tetrads have the same sum;
3 squares have the same sum;
both sums equal.

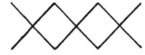

46. Numbers 1 to 11.
Six equal linear triad sums.
Find all possible basic solutions.

47. Numbers 1 to 12.
Six linear tetrads and a central square all have the same sum.

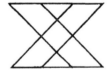

48. Numbers 1 to 20.
11 linear tetrads and each of two squares without a diagonal all have the same sum.

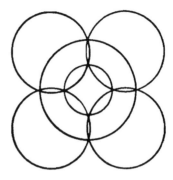

49. Numbers 1 to 8.
Each set of four in a circle has
the same sum.

50. Numbers 1 to 8.
Four equal linear triad sums and one square
sum double the other. Two solutions.

51. Numbers 1 to 8.
Four equal linear triad sums and one square
sum double the other. Two solutions.

52. Numbers 1 to 12.
Four equal linear tetrad sums and four equal dyad
sums.

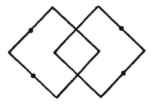

53. Numbers 1 to 14.
Eight equal linear triad sums.

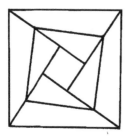

54. Numbers 1 to 12.
Every four in a line or forming a
square have the same sum.

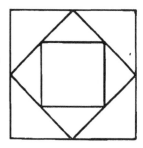

55. Twelve integers of minimum sum in which
the eight linear triads have the same sum,
and the three squares have the same sum.

56. In Ex. 55, accomplish the same result with twelve different primes.

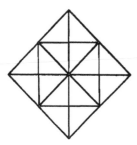

57. 13 primes of minimum sum in which each
of the ten squares shall have the same sum.

58. In the figure of Ex. 57, distribute 13 distinct primes of minimum sum
so that the ten linear triads have the same sum and the two linear pentads
have the same sum.

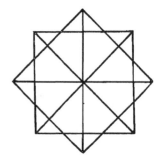

59. Numbers 1 to 25.
12 linear pentads have the same sum.

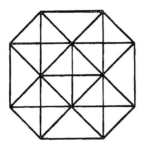

60. Numbers 1 to 17.
Fourteen squares have the same sum.

61. Using the figure of Ex. 1, obtain the same result with seven distinct primes with the smallest sum greater than 100.

62. Numbers 1 to 13.
Twelve equal linear triad sums.
Find all solutions.

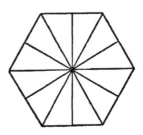

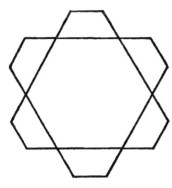

63. Numbers 1 to 18.
6 outer pairs have the same sum, and
6 linear tetrads have the same sum.

64. Numbers 1 to 10.
Six equal square sums.

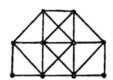

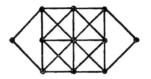

65. Numbers 1 to 11.
Eight equal square sums.

99

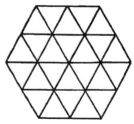

66. Numbers 1 to 19.
Six equal linear triad sums;
six equal linear tetrad sums;
three equal linear pentad sums.

67.

1873	1910	1882
1901	1940	1919
1927	1938	1891

Nine coins have these dates.
Can they be arranged so as to
form a magic 3-square?

68. Complete this magic square.

130			58
	78	69	180
103			
	17		60

69. Complete this magic square.

	100	90	
80		83	
70	55		91
			76

70. Complete this magic square.

87	94		111
		79	
56			82
	68	115	

71. Rearrange these 16 numbers
so as to form a magic square.

23	47	48	52
58	60	76	78
81	90	107	118
123	125	136	146

72. Complete this magic square.

43			
		17	
21		9	19
25	6		28

73. Complete this magic square.

	36		35
19		37	
41		39	
80		60	

143			231
		103	
187		155	Y
X	141		160

74. Complete this magic square, given that X + Y = 190.

200			125
	98		107
100	117		
	A	B	

75. Complete this magic square, given that A exceeds B by 79 and the sum of all the numbers is 1948.

76. In the text we found a solution in prime numbers with a minimum sum for the magic 3-square. Find a solution with minimum sum if 1 is excluded from the list of prime numbers.

77. Form two magic 3-squares with eighteen different prime numbers with minimum sum.

78. Form three magic 3-squares with twenty-seven different prime numbers with minimum sum.

285	167		200
301	237		
211		B	
A		193	

79. Complete this magic square, given that twice A exceeds B by 243.

80. Change the fewest of these numbers so as form a magic square.

6	41	73	23
19	53	37	35
68	36	20	22
50	16	15	64

81.

1	2	3	5	8	10
11	13	14	15	16	18
21	22	23	24	25	30

Arrange these eighteen numbers so as to form two magic three-squares.

82. Find ten integers of minimum sum so that the three on each of the outer triangles shall have the same sum.

82a. Construct a cross-pentagon with minimum sum of all the numbers.

82b. Find a second solution to Ex. 82a.

82c. Construct a cross-pentagon with ten different primes with minimum sum.

83. Numbers 1 to 10.
Five equal linear triad sums;
outer pentagon sum exceeds inner pentagon sum by 5.

84. Numbers 1 to 11.
Two pentagonal sums equal;
five linear triad sums equal.

85. In the cross-hexagon we considered in the text, find an additional solution in the case where we use consecutive integers and require the six outer triangles to have the same sum.

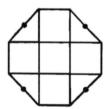

86. Numbers 1 to 16.
Five equal square sums;
four equal linear triad sums.

87. Numbers 1 to 16.
The eight linear tetrads and also
the two inner and outer squares all
have the same sum.

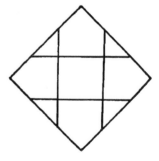

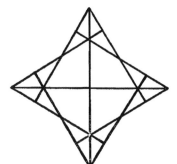

88. Numbers 1 to 21.
Ten equal linear pentad sums.

89. Numbers 1 to 24.
Four equal linear triad sums;
the nine squares and the four linear
tetrads all have the same sum.

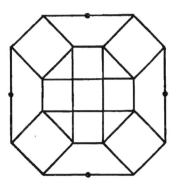

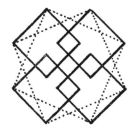

90. Numbers 1 to 24.
Eleven equal square sums.

91. Leaving the four indicated numbers in
position, distribute the remaining numbers
from 1 to 15, one in each circle, so that:
a) Every column has the same sum;
b) every row has the same sum.

103

92.

1	2	3	4	5
6	7	8	9	10
11	12	13	14	15

Rearrange these fifteen numbers so that:

a) In each column the middle number is the mean of the other two;

b) the top row of numbers increases from left to right;

c) the difference between the top and bottom numbers of any column is not duplicated.

93. Use the numbers from 1 to 18 to form two magic 3-squares in which the total of the numbers in one exceeds by 9 that of the numbers in the other.

65 : 80	68	77	46 : 33
49 : 63	11	38	16 : 111
35 : 57	4	48	76 : 34
15 : 61	66	101	82 : 17
75 : 58	62	22	73 : 28
32 : 5	37	85	42 : 21

94. This represents an array of domino-like blocks. Can they be rearranged so as to form a magic six-square?

95. This represents an array of ordinary dominoes. The problem is to fill in the proper pips so that the total of each of the seven rows will be the same and the total of each of the eight columns will be the same.

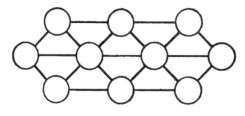

96. Distribute the numbers from 1 to 10, one in each circle, so that the sum of the nineteen differences of each pair connected directly by a line segment shall be:

a) a minimum;

b) a maximum.

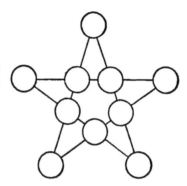

97. Distribute the numbers from 1 to 10, one in each circle, so that the sum of the fifteen differences of pairs connected directly by line segments shall be:
a) a minimum;
b) a maximum.

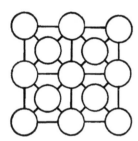

98. Distribute the numbers from 1 to 13, one in each circle, so that the sum of the 28 differences of pairs connected directly by straight line segments shall be:
a) a minimum;
b) a maximum.

99. Solve the problem in the text regarding cross-hexagons for integers having a minimum sum without requiring that the six line tetrad sums be equal.

100. Do the same with primes having a minimum sum.

101. Form a magic four-square with sixteen different prime numbers having the smallest possible total.

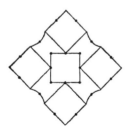

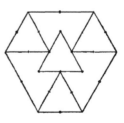

102. Numbers 1 to 40.
24 equal linear triad sums.

103. 1 to 24.
15 equal triad sums.

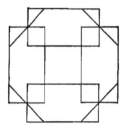

104. 1 to 32.
  8 equal tetrads.
 12 equal triads.

105. 1 to 48.
24 equal tetrad sums.

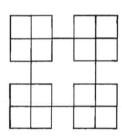

106. 1 to 36.
21 equal square sums.
 4 equal linear hexad sums.

107. 1 to 46.
18 equal tetrad sums.
 3 equal heptad sums.

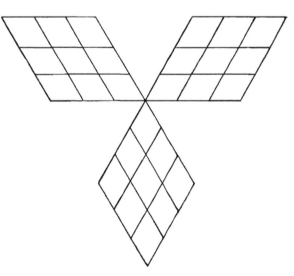

VII LINE PROBLEMS

General

Many problems concern themselves with lines as such. Of course they may, and generally do, involve arithmetical, algebraical and geometrical considerations. However, in this brief chapter, we shall stress several questions which involve lines *per se* essentially.

Networks

Suppose we have a linear figure which we can draw in one continuous broken or curved line. This is equivalent to assuming that the path can be traversed without duplicating any part of it in one continuous motion. Now suppose also that we have another, closed, path that can be drawn in one continuous line. Now if we superimpose the second upon the first it follows that the combined figure can be traced in one continuous line. Suppose A be one of the points in common. We begin to trace the first figure till we arrive at A. Here we interrupt the drawing of the first figure while we trace the second figure completely and then continue on to complete the first figure. Obviously, this presupposes that where we have a closed figure that can be drawn in one continuous line, any point upon it may be taken as the initial and terminal point of the drawing. From this consideration we decide that if a path can be drawn in one continuous motion of a point and we superimpose a number of closed paths on it so that no two parts of the compound figure are unconnected with each other, then the combined figure can be traced in one continuous line.

In general, too, this may be accomplished without the path crossing itself. Here paths may arrive at and proceed from a common point without actually crossing.

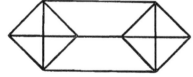

Consider the network alongside: Can that be traced in one continuous stroke? We note three closed paths, two squares and one rectangle that may be conceived as superimposed on the remainder of the figure; the long horizontal straight line through the middle of the figure. Since the latter can obviously be traced in one continuous motion, we deduce as above that the entire figure can.

This implies that we start the tracing at one end of the long horizontal line and finish at the other. We ask: Is that necessary? Will any other point of intersection do? Let us see. Suppose we consider a point at which we neither start nor finish. That point has a certain number of lines emanating from it. We observe, though, that for every line by which we approach and reach that point there is another distinct line by means of which we leave. Hence such a point must have an *even* number of lines radiating from it. In the case we are considering there are two points with an *odd* number of lines emanating from each. Hence neither point is one that is not a starting or finishing point. Therefore we must start and finish at these points.

Suppose that all points have an even number of lines meeting at each. In that case it does not matter which point we start at.

Now suppose that there are more than two points at each of which an odd number of lines meet. Then from the discussion above it is clear that

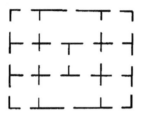

a single transit without duplication of any part of the path is impossible. A little consideration will show that there must be an even number of such points. The question arises: How many strokes are required then? The answer is: Half as many strokes as there are points of that category.

Our findings about any figure hold good even if the lines are twisted about. If the lines be conceived of as flexible

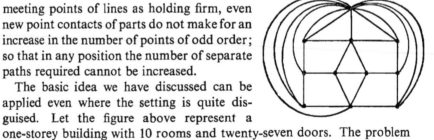

and elastic but unbreakable wire, and the meeting points of lines as holding firm, even new point contacts of parts do not make for an increase in the number of points of odd order; so that in any position the number of separate paths required cannot be increased.

The basic idea we have discussed can be applied even where the setting is quite disguised. Let the figure above represent a one-storey building with 10 rooms and twenty-seven doors. The problem

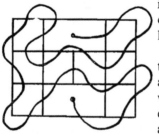

is to go through all the doors, each once only, on a single trip. Can it be done, and, if so, how?

For our purpose, we shall regard each of the ten rooms as a point, represented, say, by a dot at its centre. We shall regard each doorway as a path connecting any two points. The entire outdoors will be represented by a dot anywhere without, say at the top. In the next figure we represent by a line between two points the doorway connecting the rooms they represent. Each of the four corner points has two lines connecting it with the outdoor point. In all, as expected, we have here

27 connecting lines. This now looks familiar. We have two, and only two, points of odd order. Hence we must start and finish at one of these. In other words, our transit through all the 27 doors is possible only if we start in one of the two larger rooms and finish in the other.

A typical solution is shown in the last drawing on page 108.

It will be noted that our discussion holds good for three (and higher) dimensions as well.

One-way paths

We refer again to our brief discussion in Chapter III. Two points are to be stressed: First, where a point X can be arrived at directly from one of a series of points A, B, C, $\cdots$, then if a, b, c, $\cdots$, are the numbers of ways, respectively, of arriving at A, B, C, $\cdots$, the total number of ways of arriving at X is $a + b + c + \cdots$. Continuing pointwise in this way, we finally obtain the total number of ways of arriving at the final point along the given network of one-way paths.

Again, this may be worked backwards. We ask at each point: In how many ways can we finish from here? Clearly, that is the sum of the numbers attached to each of the points which may be reached from the given point along the one-way paths of the network. Otherwise, too, the number of ways of going from A to B must be the same as for those going from B to A.

Counting areas

Suppose we look at the adjoining figure and ask: Into how many pieces has the ellipse been cut by the criss-crossing curvilinear line? Well, there is no trouble in counting them. Now suppose that several such lines are

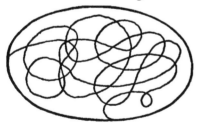

superimposed on the same figure. Counting becomes difficult, not because of the larger number reached, but because of the considerable likelihood of overlooking or duplicating some of the irregularly-situated areas. However, a method of merely counting will give the correct figure without eyestrain or uncertainty, or the detailed procedure of numbering each area sequentially.

Suppose we trace the entire figure. Let us start at any point on the ellipse and trace that figure (though convenient, this is not essential). We count an additional 1 every time the moving point meets that part of its path already traced. So we count 1 on completing the ellipse. The point

109

now moves along the ellipse till it reaches a branching-off point and we continue to trace the twisted curvilinear line. As soon as the moving point first meets its path we count 1 more, to 2, and proceed. In this way we count each area defined until the figure is completed. For a superimposed figure we still start in the same way, then branch off from any intersecting point and continue counting. Thus a tracing of the figure will enable one to count the distinct areas without annoyance.

A somewhat similar procedure will enable us to count line segments.

Alignments

One of the exercises which follow concerns ten trees with five sets of four in alignment. What is the general solution to such a problem? If we consider five lines at random, subject merely to the condition that no three lines concur and no two are parallel, we get ten points of intersection and five sets of four in a line. Bearing this in mind, other solutions may be found.

Similar questions arise with or about lines. For example, given n points (these may just as readily be taken in space), how many distinct triangles may be formed? The answer will depend on the number of collineations of three or more points, and the number of each type.

Or else, given n lines in a plane, how many distinct triangles are formed? This will depend, first, on the number of instances of parallel lines, and how many lines are parallel in each case; second, on the number of concurrences of three or more lines and the number of lines so meeting in each case.

A similar problem is that of determining the number of tetrahedra formed by n planes. This will depend on the number of sets of parallel planes, the number of instances of three or more planes with a line in common, the number of instances of four or more concurrent planes, the number of each type, the possible effect of planes in more than one of these categories, etc. Again, we have the counterpart: Given n points in space, how many distinct tetrahedra are determined by four of these points?

Comments on Exercises

6. See SM for March 1953, pp. 79/80.
15. This can be done without the paths crossing.
16. Cf. Ex. 15.
21. Of course, there are many answers.
24. Conceive the square opened up at the edges and flattened out. There are thus three paths of equal length.
25. Cf. Ex. 24, but try that in three ways.
29. The total number of ways mounts surprisingly fast.

38. The writer has five distinct methods.
41. There are four solutions all told.

Exercises

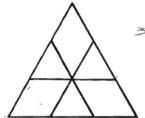

1. How many strokes are required to make this figure?

2. How many strokes are required to form this figure?

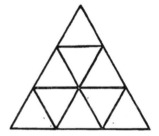

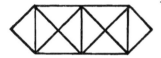

3. How many strokes?

4. It is impossible to draw this figure in one continuous line, but it becomes possible on adding one more stroke to the figure. Having done that, in how few straight strokes may the figure be completed?

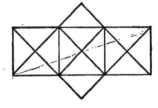

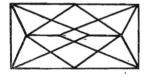

5. Draw in one line to make transit in one continuous line possible.

111

6. Omit one stroke so as to make the remainder possible of transit in one continuous trip.

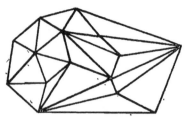

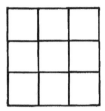

7. How many continuous strokes are required?

8. How many are required here?

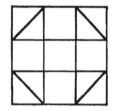

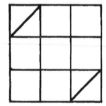

9. And how many here?

10. This represents a cubic wire frame. How few separate strands will form it?

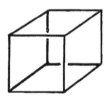

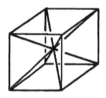

11. How many here?

12. And how many here?

13. In Ex. 10, if the diagonals are added in each of the six faces, how many strokes are then required?

14. In Ex. 10, if every vertex is connected with each of the others by a straight strand, how many separate pieces of wire will suffice?

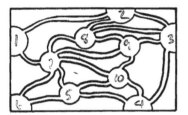

15. Go through all the park paths once on a single trip.

16. Do the same here.

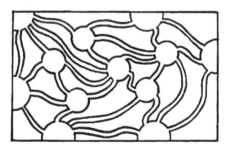

17. This represents 13 camps: Starting at any one, and returning to it, what is the shortest path that will include each of the camps?

18. In Ex. 17, if one visits each camp once, goes from one to another in a straight line, and does not cross his own path, what is the longest route?

113

19. These represent 11 camps. What is the shortest closed route that will include all of them?

20. Here again we have 13 camps. What is the shortest closed route that will include all of them?

21. Here we have 25 camps. What is the shortest closed route that will include all of them?

22. In the figure of Ex. 21, join successively two points by a straight line segment not passing through another point so as to form a broken line of six segments with a maximum total length. Here no two segments may cross.

23. This represents a rectangular field and a point within. One must reach each of the four sides of the field and return to the point along the shortest path. What is that path?

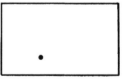

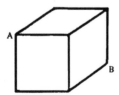

24. This represents a cube. What is the shortest path from A to B along the surface of the cube?

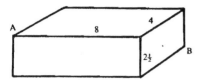

25. This represents a solid block with the dimensions indicated. What is the shortest path from A to B along the surface of the block?

26. This represents a square room with an inner square half its width walled off. The small black squares represent pillars. All the walls are covered with vertical mirrors. Where may one stand so as to see oneself all round the central square?

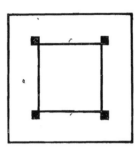

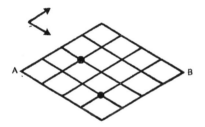

27. This represents a network of paths along which we may move only in the directions of the arrows. The two heavy dots represent blocked crossings. How many distinct paths are there from A to B?

28. This represents a lay-out of one-way roads. How many distinct paths are there from A to B?

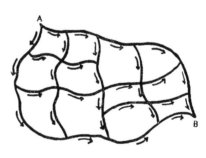

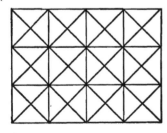

29. In this network motion proceeds only in the direction of the arrows. How many distinct paths are there from A to B?

115

30. Motion is only in the direction of the arrows. If we have *m* rows of *n* points each, how many distinct paths are there from A to B?

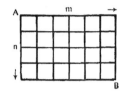

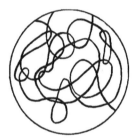

31. Into how many pieces do the lines divide the circle? Do this by inspection.

32. Into how many pieces do the lines divide this circle? (Try tracing the figure.)

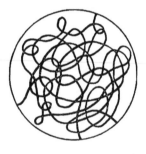

33. We have here two interwoven closed wire loops. These are cut by a circular cylindrical knife (dotted line). How many pieces of wire are obtained?

34. This circle is divided into ten equal arcs. Each of the ten points of division is connected by a straight line with each of the others.
1) How many connecting lines?
2) How many points of intersection?
3) How many of these are on 3 or more lines?
4) How many non-overlapping areas?
5) How many rectangles with vertices on circumference?

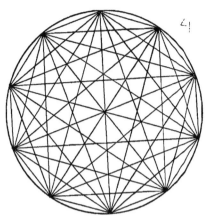

35. Arrange *n* points in a plane so that as many distinct lines as possible may be drawn to join pairs of points without intersection. How many such lines are there?

36. In Ex. 35, what is the minimum number of non-intersecting segments?

37. Connect as many pairs of these points as possible by straight lines so that no two intersect and the total length of all the lines is a maximum.

38. Draw a broken line of six segments which will go through all the 16 points.

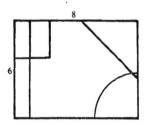

39. Find a second solution to Ex. 38.

40. This represents a thick metal block. One-eighth of the area is to be cut off. The cost varies with the length of cut. Four ways are suggested:
1. Cut a strip off the end.
2. Cut a square out of a corner.
3. Cut an isosceles triangle off one corner.
4. Cut a circular quadrant out of one corner.
Which of these is the least expensive?

117

41. These ten dots represent as many trees in a garden. The gardener managed to transplant only two of the trees so as to have five sets of four trees in a row. Show how he might have accomplished this.

42. Find a second solution to Ex. 41.

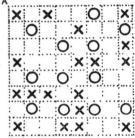

43. Starting at A, and returning to A, draw a line of minimum length along the dotted lines including all the X's and excluding all the circles.

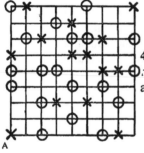

44. Starting at A, and returning to A, with no retracing, go through every X along the lines and avoid every circle.

VIII GEOMETRIC DISSECTIONS

Playing with dissections, as with other Mathematical Recreations, is good fun. Also, and frequently, problems arise for which there is no known method of solution. Indeed, many of these apparently present as much difficulty as the more famous unsolved problems of history. Possibly the future will develop methods for even these uncharted offspring of mathematical play

General theorem

We shall be concerned principally with rectilinear plane figures Concerning these we have the following general theorem:
Any plane figure bounded by straight lines, or any number of such figures together, with or without polygonal hollows, may be cu into a finite number of pieces which may be put together to form any other shape or shapes bounded by straight lines.
Steps in the proof involve the following:
1. The area, or areas, if not already such, can be cut into a finite number of pieces none of which contains a hollow.
2. Each of these may be cut into a finite number of convex polygons.
3. These may be cut into a finite number of triangles.
4. Each triangle may be cut into at most three pieces which will form a rectangle of equivalent area.
5. Each rectangle, as will be noted below, can be cut into a finite number of pieces which can be put together to form a rectangle with one dimension given.
6. These may be put together to form one rectangle.
7. This may be cut into a finite number of pieces which may be put together to form a square.
8. The same procedure may be followed with the second shape.
9. The theorem follows.
   This simple theorem apparently takes the heart out of rectilinear plane dissection problems. That indeed is true. However, in mathematical play, in dealing with mathematical puzzles as distinguished from problems, we are asked to meet special conditions to which the general theorem does not apply. For example, we may be asked to make our sections along certain lines, or with a minimum number of pieces, or to meet certain other extraneous conditions. This gives scope for considerable variety and often requires some ingenuity.
   For convenience, the author has divided dissections into various Classes, though about one or two he has but little to say.

119

Class I

In this class we put those figures which are composed of elementary squares and which are to be cut along the lines forming these squares. Even so, we shall consider three types under this heading:

Type 1

First we consider blocks of unit squares with integral dimensions a and b.

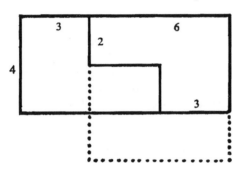

The primitive germ of the procedure is illustrated in the figure on the left, where an area 4×9 is cut into two pieces which may be put together to form a square. We notice here the formation of steps. If we have an extra step we divide the horizontal length into 4 instead of 3 equal parts and the vertical distance into 3 instead of 2 equal parts. In general, it is clear that, whatever the number of steps, we must divide one dimension into equal parts 1 greater than that into which the other dimension is divided. For definiteness, suppose $a>b$. If x be the side of the square, $a>x>b$, and $ab = x^2$. Following the step idea, if a is divided into $n + 1$ parts b is divided into n parts. Hence

$$x = \frac{n}{n+1}a = \frac{n+1}{n}b, \text{ whence } a = \left(\frac{n+1}{n}\right)^2 b.$$

Hence if such a relation holds for any integral value of n, the given rectangle may be cut into two pieces along a series of steps and put together again to form a square. That is true if the dimensions a and b are proportional to any adjacent pair of the series, 1, 4, 9, 16, 25, 36, 49, 64, 81, 100, 121, etc.

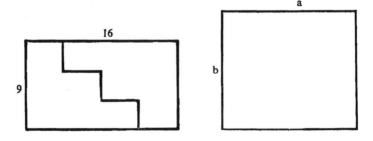

Let us consider the problem more generally. Suppose we wish to transform one given rectangle into another of the same area. Let the dimensions of the latter be x and y. Then $xy = ab$. Again, suppose our step formation divides b into n equal parts and a into $n + 1$ equal parts. Then our problem is possible if $x = \dfrac{n}{n+1}a$, whence $y = \dfrac{ab}{x} = \dfrac{n+1}{n}b$. It is also possible if $x = \dfrac{n}{n+1}b$, whence $y = \dfrac{n+1}{n}a$. Again, the problem is possible if $x = \dfrac{n+1}{n}a$ and $y = \dfrac{n}{n+1}b$, or if $x = \dfrac{n+1}{n}b$ and $y = \dfrac{n}{n+1}a$. Summing up, if x, one of the sides of the second rectangle, is equal to $\dfrac{n}{n+1}a$ or $\dfrac{n}{n+1}b$ or $\dfrac{n+1}{n}a$ or $\dfrac{n+1}{n}b$, a solution of the type considered is possible. Frequently that is so in two ways.

In any of the four cases,

$$\frac{x}{y} = \left(\frac{n+1}{n}\right)^2 \frac{a}{b} \text{ or } \left(\frac{n}{n+1}\right)^2 \frac{a}{b}.$$

Hence if such a relation is true between the proportions of the two rectangles for some integral value of n, a solution of the type discussed is possible, otherwise it is not. Conversely, given a and b, we may examine what values of n, if any, will yield permissible values for x and y.

Exercises

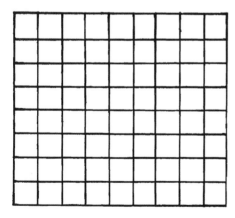

1. Cut this figure into two pieces which will fit together to form another rectangle twice as long as it is wide.

2. Find a second solution to Ex. 1.

3. Given a rectangle 56 by 64. Cut it into two pieces which will form a rectangle with its sides in the proportion 2:3.

4. In Ex. 3, find a second solution.

Type 2

This is the same as Type 1 except that we do not start with solid rectangles. The exercises themselves are sufficient illustration.

Exercises

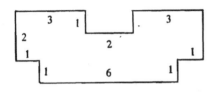

5. Cut this figure into four pieces of the same size and shape.

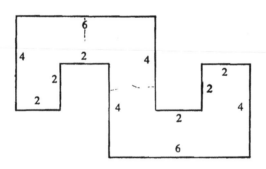

6. Cut this figure into four pieces of the same size and shape which may be put together to form a square.

7. Cut this into two pieces which will form a rectangle.

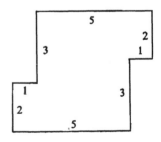

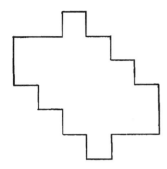

8. Cut into four pieces of the same size and shape so that they will form a Greek Cross.

9. Cut into two pieces which will form a square.

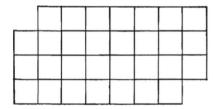

10. Cut into two pieces which will form a rectangle 5×6.

10a. Cut into three pieces which can be put together to form a square. This is a direct application of the primitive idea.

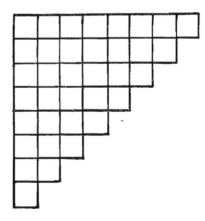

123

11. This carpet has a central square cut out. Cut the remainder into two pieces which will form a rectangle.

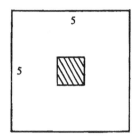

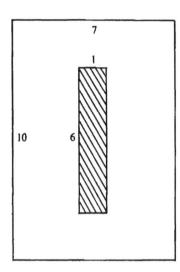

12. This carpet has a central strip cut out. Cut the remainder into two pieces which will form a square.

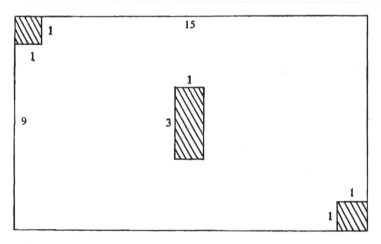

13. This carpet has a central strip cut out and also two corner pieces. Cut the remainder into two pieces which can be sewn together to form a full rectangle.

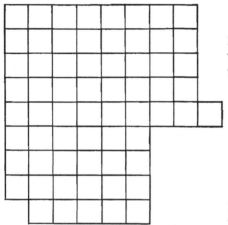

14. Cut this into three pieces which may be put together to form a square.

14a. Cut this into three pieces which may be put together to form a square.

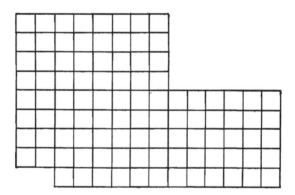

15. Cut this area into three pieces which can be put together to form a square.

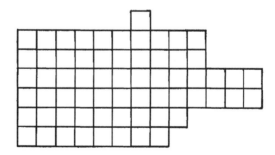

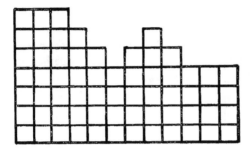

16. Cut this area into three pieces which may be put together to form a square.

Type 3

This type is the same as the previous one, except for the inclusion of quasi-geometric restrictions. As such it is very rich in possibilities. We shall comment on three problems included in the Exercises which follow.

Exercises 17 and 18 suggest the more general problem: Given a rectangle m × n with m and n commensurable, what is the minimum number of whole squares into which it may be cut? To the writer this seems to be a very difficult problem—he has not even attempted a general solution. However, we must recognize that many problems of apparently staggering difficulty do give way before a sustained attack and often in a quite primitive way. Time only will tell.

Suppose we now consider Exercises 25 and 26, and seek a method of procedure. A little reflection will show that no piece will contain two corner square cells, and the four pieces must therefore be such that each will fit into another if turned through 90° about the centre of the large square. It follows then that the four central square cells must belong to different pieces, and so we may indicate as part of the dividing cuts two cross lines at the centre dividing these four square cells. Again, in Ex. 25, the two 1's at the top must be separated by a cutting line. Now this cutting line of unit length must occur also in the three other positions of the figure where a turn of 90° about the centre of the large square will place it successively. The same thing is true for every other instance where the same number appears in adjacent squares. If we now include all such partial cuts the solution is readily obtained, and is seen to be unique.

In the case of Ex. 21, and the several similar ones with it, a like idea may be applied. Here we are required to cut the larger square into four pieces of the same size and shape, each containing an X. Applying the same ideas as in the 8 × 8 square we have discussed, we have a central cross of cuts consisting of two lines each two units long, and one unit cut in four positions. We proceed as follows: First repeat the drawing three times. Now we can continue from an extremity of the central cross in three different directions for an additional unit cut. In each case such cut is represented in the other three symmetric positions. Each of these cases is again subdivided and continued till we get a solution or a contradiction. In this case the solution is unique.

An interesting problem

This suggests a different type of question: Suppose the 6×6 has no marks in it, and we are required to cut it into four pieces of the same size and shape. How many different shapes are there? Here again we follow the ideas applied to the previous problems. First, assuming that each of the four pieces when turned through 90° about the centre of the 6×6 is congruent to another, we start with two cuts across each other and consider all cases by continuing these cuts in all possible directions. Following this out, we get 50 distinct shapes.

However, in this case we have to consider possibilities that do not apply to the other problems. In the first place, a single piece *may* contain two corner square cells. Secondly, a half square, 3×6, may be cut into two pieces of the same size and shape. Suppose we consider the upper half of the square, with the cells numbered. If the half square, with cells numbered from 1 to 18, is to be cut into two pieces of the same size and shape, they must be congruent if one is turned about 180°. Hence it is obvious that the cutting line must divide cells 9 and 10. Again, starting with this cut of unit length, and subdividing for all possibilities, we get an additional number of shapes, 23, one of which, a 3×3 square, is identical with one we have already formed. Following out this procedure in detail, we get a total of 72 different shapes.

1	2	3	4	5	6
7	8	9	10	11	12
13	14	15	16	17	18
19	20	21	22	23	24
25	26	27	28	29	30
31	32	33	34	35	36

The numbered 6×6 figure indicates one possible dissection. In the following list, we give all possible shapes resulting from our method of procedure. In each we refer to the numbered squares, the nine associated numbers indicating a set of numbered cells producing the shape in question, but not necessarily in that position. The upper two are symmetric with themselves. In the other cases, pairs which are mirror images of each other are on the same line:

1.2. 3. 7. 8. 9.13.14.15
1.7. 8.13.14.15.19.20.25
1.2. 7. 8.13.14.19.20.21   1.2. 3. 7. 8.13.14.19.20
1.2. 7. 8.13.14.15.19.20   1.2. 7. 8. 9.13.14.19.20
1.2. 3. 4. 5.10.11.16.17   1.7.13.19.20.21.25.26.27

1.7. 8. 9.13.14.15.19.20	1.2. 7. 8. 9.13.14.15.19
1.7. 8. 9.13.14.15.19.25	1.7.13.14.15.19.20.21.25
2.3. 7. 8. 9.13.19.25.26	1.2. 7.13.19.20.21.26.27
3.7. 8. 9.13.19.20.25.26	1.2. 7. 8.13.19.20.21.27
1.7. 9.13.14.15.19.25.26	1.2. 7.13.14.15.19.21.25
1.3 7. 8. 9.13.19.20.25	1.7. 8.13.19.20.21.25.27
1.2. 7. 8.13.14.15.19.25	1.7.13.14.15.19.20.25.26
1 2. 3. 7. 8.13.14.20.21	2.3. 7. 8.13.14.19.20.21
1.7. 8.13.14.19.20.21.25	1.7. 8. 9.13.14.19.20.25
7 8.13.14.15.19.25.26.27	1.2. 3. 7.13.14.15.20.26
2.7. 8.13.14.15.19.25.26	1.2. 7.13.14.15.19.20.26
1.7.13.14.19.20.21.25.26	1.2. 7. 8. 9.13.14.19.25
2.7. 8. 9.13.14.19.20.21	1.2. 3. 7. 8.13.14.15.20
1.2. 7.13.14.19.20.21.26	2.7. 8. 9.13.14.19.25.26
1.2. 3. 7.13.14.20.21.26	2.8. 9.13.14.19.25.26.27
1.2. 7. 8. 9.10.13.15.19	1.7. 9.13.14.15.16.19.20
1.2. 3. 4. 7. 9.13.19.25	1.7.13.19.21.25.26.27.28
1.7. 8. 9.10.13.15.19.25	1.7.13.15.19.20.21.22.25
2.3. 8.13.14.19.20.21.22	1.7.10.13.14.15.16.19.20
1.2. 3. 4. 7.10.13.19.25	1.7.13.19.22.25.26.27.28
1.7. 8. 9.10.13.16.19.25	1.7.13.16.19.20.21.22.25
1.7.10.11.13.14.15.16.17	1.2. 3. 4. 5. 7 10 11.13
1.2. 3. 4. 5. 7. 9.11.13	1.7. 9.11.13.14.15.16.17
1.2. 7. 8.10.13.14.15.16	1.2. 3. 4. 7. 8.10.13.14
1.2. 3. 4. 5. 6. 8. 9.12	1.2. 3. 4. 5. 6. 7.10.11
1.2. 3. 4. 5. 6. 9.11.12	1.2. 3. 4. 5. 6. 7. 8.10
1.2. 3. 4. 5. 6. 8.10.12	1.2. 3. 4. 5. 6. 7. 9.11
1.7. 8. 9.13.14.15.16.17	1.2. 3. 4. 5. 7. 8. 9.13
1.7. 8.10.13.14.15.16.17	1.2. 3. 4. 5. 7. 8.10.13
1.2. 7.10.11.13.14.15.16	1.2. 3. 4. 7.10.11.13.14
1.2. 7. 8. 9.13.14.15.16	1.2. 3. 4. 7. 8. 9.13.15
1.2. 3. 4. 5. 6.10.11.12	1.2. 3. 4. 5. 6. 7. 8. 9

If we consider a shape identical with its mirror image, we have then obviously only 37 different shapes.

It is readily seen that in a 4×4 we have 8 distinct shapes. This suggests possible formulas for a $2n \times 2n$ structure, and offers what appears to be a very difficult problem for a more general analysis.

Exercises

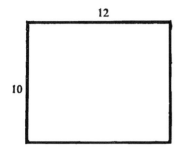

12

10

17. Given a rectangle 10×12. Divide it into the fewest number of whole squares.

13

11

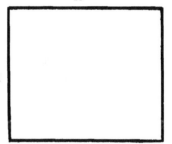

18. Given a rectangle 11×13. Divide it into the fewest squares.

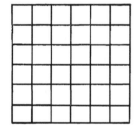

19. Cut this area along the lines into the greatest number of different shapes.

20. Cut this figure into four pieces of the same size and shape so that each piece contains an A and no piece contains either two corner squares or a 2×2 square.

129

21. Cut this figure into four pieces of the same size and shape each containing one X.

22. Cut this figure into four pieces of the same size and shape each containing one X.

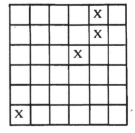

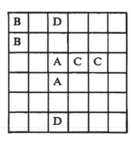

23. Cut each square into two pieces so that all four pieces will have the same size and shape and will contain one each of the letters A, B, C, D.

24. Cut this figure along the lines into two pieces of the same size (both containing 18 square cells) so that each piece will contain one each of the numbers from 1 to 8.

25. Cut this figure along the lines into four pieces of the same size and shape each containing one each of the figures from 1 to 4. (See SM June 1952, p. 112.)

		2				1	1
	1	2					
	1			4	4		
	3	3			3	3	
		4	4				
	2	2					

26. Do the same as with Ex. 25.

1	2	3	4	5	6	7	8
9	10	11	12	13	14	15	16
17	18	19	20	21	22	23	24
25	26	27	28	29	30	31	32
33	34	35	36	37	38	39	40
41	42	43	44	45	46	47	48
49	50	51	52	53	54	55	56
57	58	59	60	61	62	63	64

27. Cut this figure along the lines into two pieces of the same size and shape in such a way that the sum of the numbers in each shall be the same.

28. In Ex. 27, cut the figure into four pieces of the same size (each containing 16 square cells) in which the sum of the numbers in each shall be the same.

Class II

In this class we include rectilinear figures cut on the bias. This too we shall consider under three types.

Type 1

This will include figures composed of a few elementary squares and other figures of equivalent character.

At this point we note several elementary considerations.

We observe that every triangle may be cut into three pieces which can be put together to form a rectangle. The first figure overleaf shows how. This figure is general, since every triangle has at least two acute angles. Also, every parallelogram may be cut into pieces which may be put together to form a rectangle with one side fixed. The adjoining figure

131

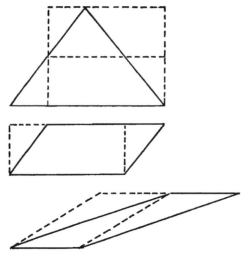

shows how that is accomplished in two pieces where the perpendicular from the end of the first side cuts the opposite side. Where such is not the case the next figure shows how the given parallelogram may be cut into two pieces which may be put together so as to bring the perpendicular to the base from an extremity nearer to the opposite side. The last procedure may be repeated till the preceding case is arrived at. Of course, other methods also will apply.

By an application of the last result it may be shown that any rectangle may be cut into a finite number of pieces which may be put together to form a rectangle with one side given. A more direct method will be explained under Type 2.

These simple ideas are the basis for the general theorem we discussed at the beginning of this chapter.

Let us consider the sort of procedure we follow to solve a problem in

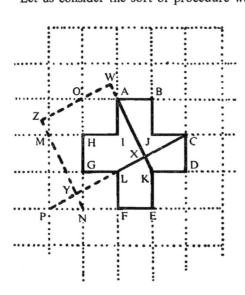

this classification: Suppose a figure is to be cut into pieces to form a square. First we count the elementary squares which constitute the figure. Suppose that to be 8. Then the side of the square we wish to obtain is $\sqrt{8}$, or $2\sqrt{2}$. Hence two diagonal lengths of a square cell give the side of our final square. So we may expect to cut our figure along two diagonal lengths somewhere. But will that suffice? Suppose we have two such diagonal cuts of unit squares. Each of them yields on each side a diagonal length. Thus the two cuts yield 4 such unit diagonal lengths. But the final figure requires two of them to a side, i e. 8 such diagonal lengths. So we must seek to make such additional cuts.* Furthermore, we must look for a way to make the second cuts at right angles to the first. The reason is that the final figure has not only four sides, but also four right angled vertices, and these four right angles must be provided. Two intersecting diagonal cuts will produce such vertices.

Let us apply similar ideas to that ancient plaything, the Greek cross. This is composed of 5 elementary squares. If the final figure is a square, its side must be $\sqrt{5}$. This is represented by the line from A to C, or from A to K, etc. Suppose we draw the square ACEG. Obviously, the corner piece at B can fill in the hollow at J, the corner at D the hollow at K, etc. This then yields a solution. It will be noted that in placing each piece that has been lopped off it has been turned about 180°. However, if the corner at B fills in the hollow at L, and the others similarly, there is translation but no rotation. That characteristic is found in the solution of many problems of this type. Our solution has the advantage of symmetry. However, suppose we require that only 4 pieces be used. What then?

Suppose we try again. But, first, suppose the cross to be located in a field of elementary squares of which it covers 5. Let us try another cut on the bias. Suppose we try one along AK This has the length $\sqrt{5}$ and yields the equivalent of two sides of our desired square. We need then another such cut, or two such cuts on elementary squares. Where shall we now cut? From our discussion of the case with 8 cells, we must look for a similar cut at right angles to AK. Where shall that be? Suppose we try LC, cutting AK in X. This at least yields the proper perimeter length and the four vertices at X. But will the four pieces fit into a square of area 5? To test that, let us leave one of the pieces, say AG, in position, and move the others. Remembering that X is to be a vertex of our final square, XL must be prolonged till it has the length $\sqrt{5}$ But CX + XL = $\sqrt{5}$. Hence the prolongation has the length CX, and that suggests we move one of the pieces on the right. Taking the piece AC, we note that it fits into the position ML. Similarly, the piece FX fits into the position HW, X falling on W, on the prolongation of XA. The piece KC then fits in the position MO, with X falling on Z, the prolongation of NM. We thus have a solution in four pieces.

Observe that LY lands on a vertex P of the network of elementary squares. Suppose we now conceive that network as being overlapped by another consisting of elementary squares which include XYZW. Having done that, the fact that our particular choice of cuts yields a solution becomes obvious.

---

* It will be seen that this does not apply to Type 2.

In this case we observe also that the three pieces we moved were not rotated. Further, we note that DC in the new position falls along HO, and so does FL. Again, we note that the piece KC would fit into the position NL. Then we could have accomplished our result as follows: We could have moved the two pieces AC and CK rigidly together to the position MHGLFN; then we could have moved the combined piece YXKEN to the position ZWAIM. Now let us consider the figure before we make the second move. We have the figure MIAKEN cut by YX ⊥ AX. Clearly it does not matter where YX is, as long as it does not go past the point I. In other words, the cut YXC could be taken parallel to itself in any position from where it is to that where it includes the point I. Any such position will yield a solution in four pieces. Again, we began the first move by taking the combined block ABJCDK and moving it rigidly at right angles to AK. Clearly AK could also be taken in any position parallel to itself from AK up to the position where it includes the point J or the point L. Thus there are an infinitude of solutions in four pieces. It will be noted that such non-rotational sliding shifts often retain a design which may be supposed to cover the area cut.

In cases where the figure includes 10 square cells, the side of the final square is HD. A simple adaptation may be made for other cases.

Comments on Exercises

62a. This is a direct application of the discussion in the text.

65. It will be noted that this involves a demonstration of the Pythagorean Theorem.

66. It will be seen that this is equivalent to Ex. 64.

67 and **68.** These are equivalent to Ex. 65.

69. Like Ex. 65, this also serves as a demonstration of the Pythagorean Theorem.

74. It may be noted that this figure is equivalent to a set of elementary squares with one set of parallel diagonals.

78. Actually, this can be done with three pieces.

80. This is equivalent to Ex. 9. (See SM for March 1952; p. 304.)

81. This is equivalent to Ex. 10.

Exercises

29. Cut this figure into three pieces which will form a square.

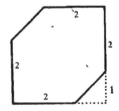

30. Show how to cut the hollow octagon into three pieces which will form the cross.

31. Cut the remains of the mat into five pieces which will form a square retaining the design.

32. Cut this area into 4 pieces which will form a square.

33. Four pieces. Form a square.

34. Four pieces: Square.

35. Four pieces: Square.

36. Find a second solution to Ex. 35.

135

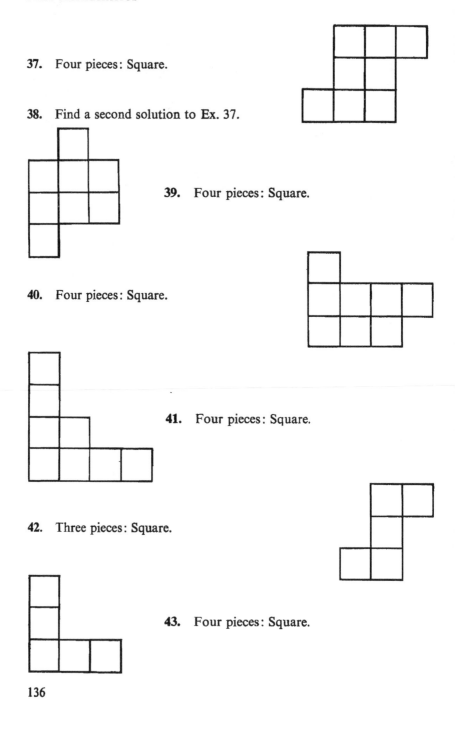

37. Four pieces: Square.

38. Find a second solution to Ex. 37.

39. Four pieces: Square.

40. Four pieces: Square.

41. Four pieces: Square.

42. Three pieces: Square.

43. Four pieces: Square.

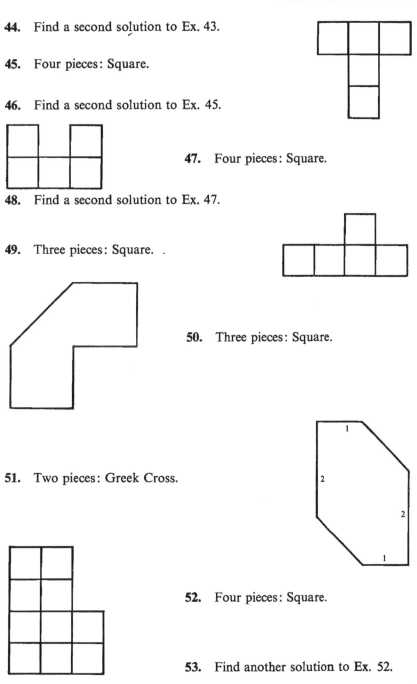

44. Find a second solution to Ex. 43.

45. Four pieces: Square.

46. Find a second solution to Ex. 45.

47. Four pieces: Square.

48. Find a second solution to Ex. 47.

49. Three pieces: Square.

50. Three pieces: Square.

51. Two pieces: Greek Cross.

52. Four pieces: Square.

53. Find another solution to Ex. 52.

137

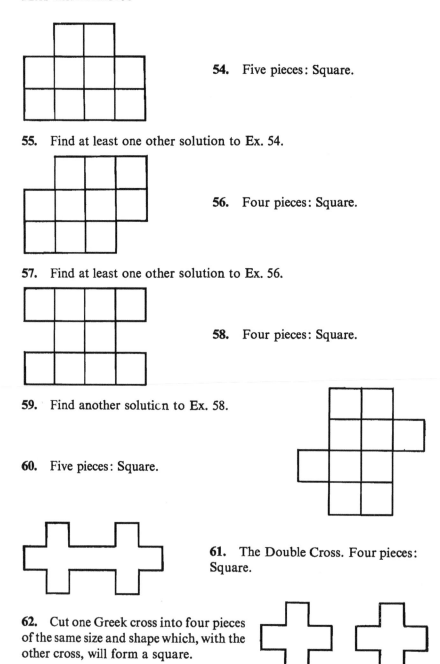

54. Five pieces: Square.

55. Find at least one other solution to Ex. 54.

56. Four pieces: Square.

57. Find at least one other solution to Ex. 56.

58. Four pieces: Square.

59. Find another solution to Ex. 58.

60. Five pieces: Square.

61. The Double Cross. Four pieces: Square.

62. Cut one Greek cross into four pieces of the same size and shape which, with the other cross, will form a square.

62a. Cut a Greek Cross into four pieces of the same size and shape which can be put together to form a square.

63. Cut a rectangle 1×2 into three pieces which will form a Greek Cross. (See AMM for August-September 1926; p. 388.)

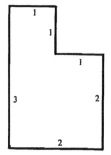

64. Three pieces: Square.

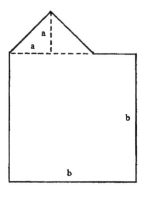

65. Three pieces: Square.

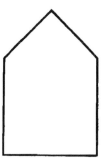

66. Three pieces: Square.

67. Three pieces: Square.

139

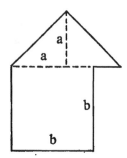

68. Here a ≤ b. Three pieces: Square. (See SM March 1948, p.16.)

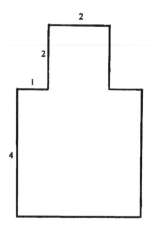

69. Given any two squares. Show how to cut the larger into four pieces of the same size and shape which, with the other, will form a square.

70. Five pieces: Square.

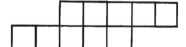

71. Four pieces: Square.

72. Three pieces: Square.

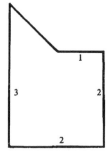

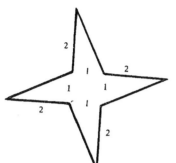

73. Five pieces: Square.

74. Cut this figure along the lines into the greatest number of different shapes.

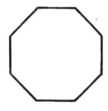

75. Cut one octagon into eight pieces which, with the other, will form an eight-pointed star.

76. Cut this into four pieces of the same size and shape.

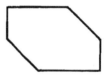

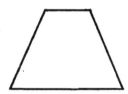

77. In this isosceles trapezoid the two diagonals are at right angles and each is equal to the base. Three pieces: Square.

78. Regular hexagon. Four pieces: Rhombus.

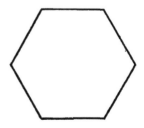

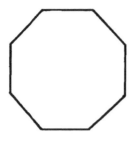

79. Regular octagon. Four pieces: Rectangle.

80. Two pieces: Square. (SM September-December 1952, p. 304.)

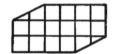

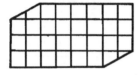

81. Two pieces: Rectangle 5×6.

Type 2

In this we put rectilinear figures with incommensurable sides.

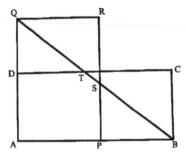

Suppose we are given the rectangle ABCD with AB = a, AD = b, and are required to cut it into pieces which will yield the rectangle APRQ, with AP = x, AQ = y, and xy = ab. We suppose a>x and b<y. For the moment we shall suppose also that

$$\frac{a}{x} = \frac{y}{b} < 2.$$

Draw BQ and consider the similar triangles formed. We have:

$$\frac{TC}{BC} = \frac{AB}{AQ}, \text{ whence } TC = \frac{b \cdot a}{y} = x = QR.$$

Also,

$$\frac{SR}{QR} = \frac{BC}{TC}, \text{ whence } SR = BC = b.$$

Hence the triangle TCB is congruent with QRS. Again, PB = a − x = DT and PS = y − b = DQ. Hence the triangle PBS is congruent with DTQ.

142

Thus we obtain our solution by cutting the rectangle ABCD into three pieces along the lines BT and PS. The two triangles cut off may then be moved into their congruent positions.

Of course, the same procedure may be applied where the sides are commensurable.

We have assumed a $\leq 2x$. This will ensure that S falls below DC. But

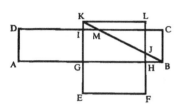

what if a $> 2x$? The procedure is best illustrated by an example. Suppose we wish to cut a rectangle 1×5 into pieces which will form a square. Here a = 5, $b = 1$, $x = y = \sqrt{5}$, and $\dfrac{a}{x} > 2$.

Let the given rectangle be ABCD. Let AG = x = $\sqrt{5}$. Cut off the rectangle AGID and place it in the position EFHG. Let EK = FL = $\sqrt{5}$. Then GK = $\sqrt{5} - 1$. Further, $\dfrac{GB}{GH} = \dfrac{5 - \sqrt{5}}{\sqrt{5}} = \sqrt{5} - 1 < 2$. We can now make the cuts BM and HJ and proceed as before.

If, similarly, A $> nx$, but $< (n + 1)x$, we cut off n $-$ 1 pieces of dimensions xb and place them one below the other starting with the position EFHG.

Applying the method here explained, we could, for example, cut an equilateral triangle into five pieces which may be reassembled to form a square of equivalent area; an otherwise troublesome matter.

This supplements the procedure explained under Class II, Type 1.

Exercises

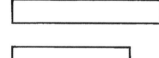

82. Cut a rectangle 1×7 into four pieces which will form a square.

83. Cut a rectangle 1×5 into as few pieces as possible which will form another rectangle twice as long as it is wide.

84. In Ex. 83, obtain a rectangle with sides in the proportion 5:6

85. In Ex. 83, obtain a rectangle with one side $\sqrt{2}$.

86. In Ex. 82, obtain a rectangle with one side $\sqrt{3}$.

Type 3

In this category we place problems with special conditions. For example, Ex. 40 of Ch. VII would be typical. We give but one exercise:

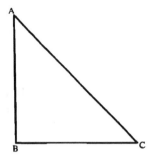

87. We are asked to cut this right-angled isosceles triangle into three equal areas by two cuts of minimum length.

Four methods are suggested:

1. Two straight line cuts $\perp$ AC.

2. Cuts from the mid-point of AC to points on CB and AB two-thirds of the way from C and A, respectively.

3. Cutting off two isosceles triangles with vertices at A and C.

4. Circular cuts with A and C as centres.

Which of these is the best?

Class III

In this we include the cutting up of solids. This field is very fruitful but largely unexplored The reasons for this are that such problems do not lend themselves readily to presentation on the printed sheet, and also generally involve acute powers of visualization. Ex. 19 of Ch. IX is an example.

Comparable to the general problem we mentioned under Type 3 of Class I is that of cutting a rectangular block with commensurable dimensions $m \times n \times r$ into the fewest number of whole cubes.

We may also inquire as to the largest number of pieces into which a sphere may be cut by n planes. Following this, we may ask: What is the largest number of pieces into which a sphere may be cut by n spherical surfaces all having the same radius as the sphere? And again: What is the largest number of pieces into which a sphere may be cut by n spheres of any radius? Also, we might ask for the general solution in three dimensions of the type of problem represented by Ex. 15 of Ch. III. It is certainly easy to ask questions!

Class IV

In this we include the cutting of lines. The writer has seen very few of these. One form requires the division of a chain of links under certain conditions. There is no reason why problems in this category cannot be created, though the writer has little to offer at this time. Ex. 33 of Ch. VII might be included here.

Exercises

88. Cut a given length into two pieces so that one is the perimeter of a square and the other of an equilateral triangle and the sum of the areas in 1) a maximum; 2) a minimum.

89. AB is a line of given length and C a fixed point on it. CB is to be cut at a point X so that the three segments of AB may serve as altitudes of a triangle. What are the limitations to the position of X? (See Ch. III.)

Class V

In this category we place the Inverse Problems. In other words, given the pieces of a cut-up, replace them to form the required figure. The exercises we append suggest the cut-up into L's we considered in Ch. III.

Though these exercises are rather simple, we wish to point out that problems or puzzles of this type can be made exceedingly difficult. We shall presently indicate a method of procedure one may apply even to these. However, several reflections on the 'simple' character of the elements we are given to work with are in order. The most complex inverse cut-up puzzle we encounter is the usual jig-saw. A normal child of eight will do these substantially as well as the average adult. Now just why is this highly complex puzzle so easy to solve? The reason is that its very complexity offers such a multiplicity of clues as to make the procedure little more than mechanical. It is the apparently 'simple' puzzle, one that offers no obvious starting point, "nothing to get hold of", that is often the most subtle and difficult. The author may here repeat a slogan of his: "Anything queer is a clue." A jig-saw puzzle is full of queer oddities of shape and colour, making the matching of pieces more or less unique.

Compare that with the checkerboard cut-up we have below. Here there are only 12 pieces, rather than hundreds, and each piece is 'simple'. In fact, the pieces are so simple that one may be matched with any other in at least one way. Yet such a puzzle may be made incomparably harder than a jig-saw of 2000 pieces. Again, suppose we take the next puzzle we offer, a still simpler one, composed of 12 unmarked blocks. Because of its 'simplicity' this puzzle is still harder than the checkerboard cut-up. The reason is that any piece can fit with any other in a multitudinous number of ways. Yet the solution may still be unique. This last type of puzzle, simple as it looks, may be made so difficult that few people anywhere may be expected to solve it!

This aspect of simplicity often leads the untrained person to certain sweeping but untenable conclusions. For example, those essentially weak at either game will class checkers as an 'inferior' game to chess, because of the simplicity of its pieces and its rules. The fact is that checkers is fully

145

as profound as chess, that many of its settings with but a few austere pieces involve not only beautiful conceptions but offer problems as difficult as anything in chess literature. The writer has found, in fact, that when explaining the rudiments of both games to beginners those of chess are grasped much more readily than those of checkers. In the latter game everything looks more or less alike to the novice, whereas in the former he senses immediate objectives. It usually takes several years of play for the ordinary person to recognize that checkers is a game of skill. Following the line of 'reasoning' referred to, we would at once characterize the study of geometry as an inferior intellectual activity because, forsooth, its 'rules' are simpler even than those of checkers!

Checkerboard cut-up puzzle

A board of alternating black and white squares is cut into a number of pieces, say 12, the cuts being along boundaries of the inner squares. The problem is to reconstruct the checkerboard from these pieces. This is generally harder than it looks! Incidentally, there is sometimes more than one solution. Suppose we start with an actual puzzle. Consider the following pieces:

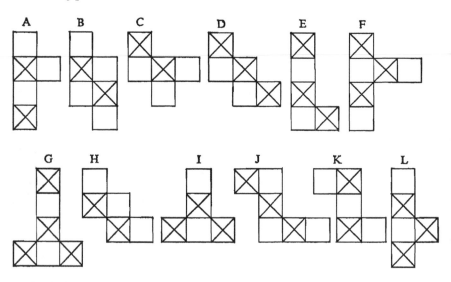

We shall suppose we have a set of cardboard pieces of larger size with the same shapes. First (as a check, of course) we count the dark and white squares to make sure there are 32 of each. We now draw a checkerboard with squares the same size—preferably a trifle larger. The work will be done on this checkerboard. Suppose the upper left hand corner is white (the standard setting). We mark each piece with a letter, as shown, from A to L.

Now the difficulty most people experience with such a puzzle—indeed with any puzzle which is not quite obvious—is due essentially to lack of system. We must recognize that almost any system is better than no system. In puzzles like these most of the puzzle skill we can exhibit goes into the choice of system. Routine labour cannot be avoided. The aim, then, is to reduce this to a minimum. We know of no short method. The tendency of the untrained or inexperienced is to keep trying various pieces at haphazard, in the hope that, somehow or other, they will hit upon the solution. The point is, by such methods a tremendous amount of duplication is possible, with the corresponding likelihood of overlooking just the combination which yields the solution. In fact, by such methods, we may even get close to the solution and give up in disgust because some small item has been overlooked.

As with many similar puzzles, we may apply the Method of Unique Exhaustion. This method, applicable to many types of problems, puzzles and 'practical' matters, consists in devising a system which, if followed through in detail, will provide for all possible combinations once and only once, so that no repetitions may occur. In other words, nothing is overlooked, and nothing is duplicated. Consequently, if there is a solution it is found, and if there are several they are all found if the exhaustion is completed. Here we must digress for an important detail:

The method of arrangements

We have often to consider questions equivalent to the following: How many five-digit numbers may be made with the digits 1, 3, 4, 6, 9, using each once in each number? Or, instead, we may inquire as to how many distinct sequences may be formed with the five letters A, B, C, D, E. For our present purpose we are not concerned with the number of sequences but with the actual writing out of all these sequences. We fix the first three letters in position and find two ways of arranging the remaining two letters. Then we replace C by D, the next letter in the Standard Sequence ABCDE, and get two more ways of completing the arrangement. Then we replace the C by E for two more, getting six arrangements. We now replace B by C, then by D, then by E, getting in each case 6 arrangements, for a total of 24. This procedure may be continued.

In applying this procedure to our puzzle we shall not actually write down our arrangements of letters, but shall do the equivalent by rapidly arranging the objects represented by these letters in all possible ways according to the system we adopt. We first arrange the twelve lettered pieces in standard order, beyond the board. The initial choice of lettering is immaterial. We shall start with piece A, and in each case work from the upper left corner of the board. Piece A fits into that in only one possible way. We next try all the possible arrangements of the other pieces with A in this position. As soon as a contradiction (impossibility) is arrived at, we go on to the next step in our arrangements. Now more pieces will fit somehow into the longer part of A placed in the upper left corner than at the top of it. Of course we choose the latter, so as to reduce the number of possibilities we have to consider. We look at piece B. This cannot fit at all at the upper right of A. Neither will C. But D will in just one way. We now have a corner that looks like the figure adjoining. Having picked two pieces (letters), we try all possible ways of fitting in the others. Again, we form the standard sequence. Once more we try that corner (indicated by arrow), which leads to the most cramped situations, and at once eliminate most remaining possibilities at a glance. Referring to the ten remaining pieces (in standard sequence), we note that B does not fit at all. C does in one way, but encloses a

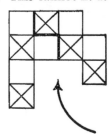

blank single square and must be discarded. Now E fits in two ways. We must try them both. First, as in the figure alongside. Here we see that only one piece fits in at the left, so we place it there without further thought. This completes the whole left side of the board. We may then attack the piece at the top, bottom, or inner corner with the remaining pieces, until every possibility leads to an impossible setting or to a solution. Even in the latter case, the procedure may be continued to make sure that either there are no other solutions or that all are found. It should be noted that as each piece is put back with the others unused it should be placed where it belongs in Standard Position. In following this procedure, it is best to keep a side memorandum as to the sequence of pieces chosen for the main positions; at least the first time the system is applied. Thus, so far as we have gone, the memorandum would be something like

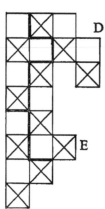

A D

E L

Of course, the written explanation is lengthy. But in actual application the arrangements thus far tried should not take more than a minute. Also, of course, for the harder types of puzzle, many thousands of arrangements may thus be reviewed. With a little practice most of these are settled at a glance, without touching a piece, only the principal initial pieces being placed. Near-solutions may occur, with but a single square projecting, where practically all the pieces will have to be placed, but that is exceptional.

To be sure, instead of looking for cramped corners to fill, we may just try all possible ways of filling a side, an adjoining side, etc. But that will require the examination of many more possibilities. The cramped corners at once eliminate most of these.

It should be noted: First, that all possible arrangements that may lead to a solution are found by this system—in fact, all solutions if the procedure is completed; second, no arrangement is duplicated—that is, there is no waste motion.

Other systems may be applied, but, whatever they are, they must have one principle in common with this system: they must all be uniquely exhaustive. As may be seen, such a system is applicable to many other types of problem.

The Block synthesis

A method similar to the last is applicable to this type of puzzle. Let us take a specific puzzle of this type for consideration, a comparatively easy one!

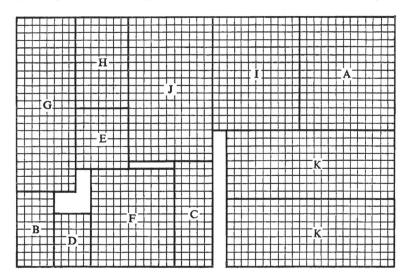

The problem is 'simply' to arrange these twelve rectangles, without overlapping or hollows, to form a rectangle. Of course, we may say

149

outright: "Where is the difficulty?" The answer may well be: "It is there because you do not see it!" As a matter of fact, though not easy, this is a comparatively simple form of this type of puzzle. This is because the relative magnitudes of the sides of the various blocks are clearly indicated by the square divisions. If these were omitted,* the first part of the problem would be to ascertain them. Let us first consider the actual problem before us: We have 12 pieces, which we have lettered from A to K for reference. We shall regard each square subdivision as a unit. Let us now look at the total area of these blocks in terms of this unit:

A	15×13	195
B	10×5	50
C	14×5	70
D	7×5	35
E	8×7	56
F	13×11	143
G	23×8	184
H	12×7	84
I	15×12	180
J	19×11	209
K	23×9	207
K	23×9	207
		1620

The total area of the rectangle we wish to obtain is, then, 1620 square units. This may be factored in various ways:

1. 12×135
2. 15×108
3. 18×90
4. 20×81
5. 27×60
6. 30×54
7. 36×45

Case 1 would just admit Piece I, but after J is put in we can go no further. Case 2 would require a piece of width 3 to fill in. That is not available.

---

* As in the CALIBRON PUZZLE, which consists of 12 accurately turned out blocks without marks or colour distinction. That degree of accuracy cannot be reproduced on the printed page, so we give the second part of the puzzle.

Similarly for Case 3. For the remaining cases, we are not yet in a position to say. We have actually four distinct problems here, and must try them all! The procedure is identical with that for the Checkerboard Cut-Up, except that the system must be applied more exhaustively before impossibilities are arrived at. This is for two reasons: First, because the pieces are not so irregular, and 'corners' which may eliminate many possibilities at once are not so readily encountered; second, because there is no distinction as to colour of adjacent squares, or as to shape either, since the side of any piece fits the side of any other piece in a variety of positions, again making for more possibilities that have to be considered. It will now begin to appear why this type of puzzle is more difficult than the previous one. To begin with, we had a rectangle measuring 20 of our units by 81. We arrange the pieces in Standard Sequence and apply the method already explained. If no solution is obtained, or if all possible ones are desired (or, what is equivalent, the assurance that there are no others), the entire procedure is repeated with another shape of rectangle, say Case 5, etc.

If the blocks have no markings at all on them, their relative dimensions must first be obtained. First, a diagram of each piece is made. Then sides of different lengths are marked separately, say with small letters. All equal side lengths are marked in the same way. That lengths are equal is judged by juxtaposition. Then different combinations of side lengths are compared by juxtaposition, and combinations that are equal are noted. This is done in various ways until we have one equation less than we have different side lengths. By these we get the relative proportions of these lengths. We may express all the others in terms of one. We then assign as many units to that one side length as will make all the other lengths integral. We may then proceed as indicated above.

Exercises

90. The dark piece of the carpet is cut out. Show how to resew the other eight pieces to form a rectangle.

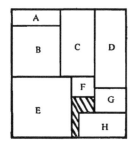

A	$36'' \times 12''$
B	$39'' \times 36''$
C	$27'' \times 51''$
D	$24'' \times 47''$
E	$45'' \times 45''$
F	$15'' \times 18''$
G	$24'' \times 18''$
H	$36'' \times 21''$

151

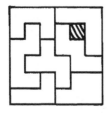

91. Cutting out the black square, resew the remainder of the mat to form a rectangle.

92. Find a second solution to Ex. 91.

93. Rearrange these seven pieces to form the second shape:

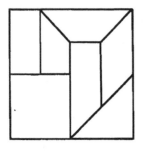

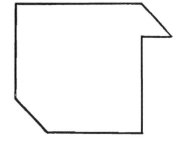

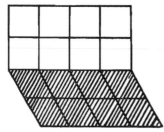

94. This represents 8 squares of cloth and as many rhombuses of another colour. For some reason, it is required to resew these 16 pieces so that, excepting at a vertex, no two pieces of the same colour may touch, and the border shall be of the same length as here indicated.

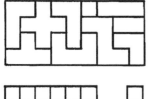

95. Rearrange these 10 pieces to form a square.

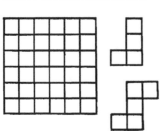

96. Cut this square along the lines in pieces of one or both the shapes shown. Note: This is based on an old European puzzle.

97. In Ex. 96, having formed the square, rearrange the same pieces to form an oblong.

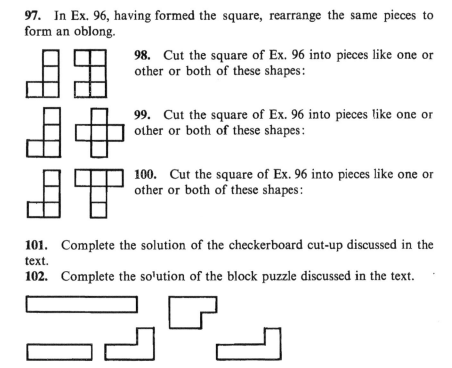

98. Cut the square of Ex. 96 into pieces like one or other or both of these shapes:

99. Cut the square of Ex. 96 into pieces like one or other or both of these shapes:

100. Cut the square of Ex. 96 into pieces like one or other or both of these shapes:

101. Complete the solution of the checkerboard cut-up discussed in the text.

102. Complete the solution of the block puzzle discussed in the text.

103. Arrange these five blocks so as to outline the letter E

Class VI

Under this we consider non-rectilinear figures.

Type 1

This includes direct problems The writer has not seen many of these. However, there is no reason why a crop of interesting puzzles or problems should not be forthcoming under this head. Exercise 104 suggests the generalization: Given a circle, what is the maximum number of pieces into which it may be cut by *n* circular arcs all having the radius of the given circle? This looks troublesome, and may be difficult.

Type 2

This includes inverse problems. This type of block composition may be even more difficult than the rectilinear block puzzle. As an illustration, suppose we are asked to reassemble the following five pieces to give a circle:

153

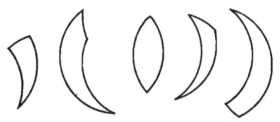

It will be noted that the cutting arcs have the same radius as the outer arcs. If care is taken to have various groups of arcs and curvilinear angles either equal or supplementary, and to cut the circle into 15, 16 or more pieces of this type, this kind of puzzle should offer the utmost difficulty. However, even then, if one is to attack such a puzzle at all, the method outlined under Class V should offer at least a chance of success in an ordinary lifetime!

Exercises

104. What is the largest number of pieces into which a circle may be cut by five arcs of the same radius as the circle?

105. What is the largest number of pieces into which a circle may be cut by five circles of any radii?

Class VII

In this category we place mixed and irregular types.

Among the few exercises which follow, Ex. 112 is particularly interesting. We may generalize the question: Given the integer n, what is the smallest rectangular area consisting of n rectangles, and no other pieces, whose $2n$ dimensions are all different integers? For n = 1 the answer is 1×2. For n = 2 there is no solution. Neither is there for n = 3 or n = 4. For n = 6, the writer has not even tried. Now, while in the mood for asking questions, why not require the $2n$ dimensions of the rectangles to be as many different prime numbers? Why not, indeed? Truly, it is easy to ask these questions, but the solutions appear to be extremely difficult!

Exercises

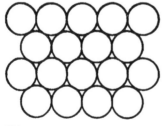

106. A contractor had engaged to cover a floor with white circular tiles as shown, the curvilinear triangular interstices to be filled by blue tiles. He estimated he would need about 120000 white tiles About how many should he order of the blue?

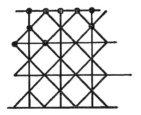

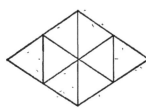

107. The same contractor had to cover a ceiling with inlaid strips of brass in the design shown, these strips being of two lengths. At each join of these strips he planned to use a brass brad. He estimated he would need about 120000 of these brads. About how many of each length of metal strip should he order?

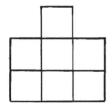

108. This represents an arrangement of sixteen matches. Remove six matches and leave two triangles. Do the same taking 7 matches, then 8, then 9, then 10. No superfluous matches are to be left over in each case. There are various solutions.

109. In Ex. 108, remove 5 matches and leave three triangles. Then do the same with 6 matches, then 7, then 8, then 9.

110. This represents an array of twenty matches. Remove 6 matches and leave three squares. Then do the same with 7 matches, then with 8, then with 9, then with 10.

111. In Ex. 21 of Ch. III, suppose the cube to be shaved *n* times. How many edges, faces and vertices would the solid then have?

112. In terms of a given unit of length, what is the smallest rectangular area composed of five rectangles of which the ten sides are all different integral measures of this unit?

IX   VISUALIZATION PROBLEMS

Of course, visualization comes into play in almost any kind of mental activity. In this brief chapter we merely select a few questions which call for the exercise of that faculty to a greater degree than elsewhere.

In stressing this characteristic, we may refer to Exercises 1, 2, 3, 4, 9, 11, 21 of Chapter III, 35, 43, 44 of Chapter VII, and 13, 15, 16, 94, 104, 105, 106, 107, 110 of Chapter VIII.

We shall touch on one or two matters briefly and close with a few exercises.

Rolling circles

We suppose, first, the circles A and B are equal. Suppose the circle B is

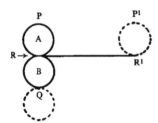

fixed while A rolls round it without slipping till it gets back to its initial position. How many revolutions has it made by then about its own axis? Consider the point P. Clearly, that point will reach the position Q, with the circle A in the dotted position below. By then, the halfway point, A has made one complete revolution about its own axis. The number of revolutions for a complete circuit is then 2.

A more effective way of regarding this type of rotation is the following (SM March-June 1950, p. 72): In the figure, suppose A rolls along the straight line to the dotted position on the right, where the distance RR′ is equal to the circumference of B. Then suppose that the line RR′ with the circle A rigidly attached and tangential to it at R′ be turned about the circle B until A gets back to its initial position. This adds one more revolution.

From this point of view it should be a simple matter to solve the Exercises from 13 to 17.

An interesting problem

This problem, as a puzzle, has become quite popular in the U.S. (See SM March-June 1954, p. 144).

The figure on the left (below) represents six discs or coins of equal size. The initial problem is to obtain the arrangement on the right from the one on the left in a minimum number of moves. A move consists

156

in sliding, without lifting, one and only one disc and, without disturbing any of the other discs, leaving it in contact with two other discs. This makes each move mechanically precise without the use of instruments.

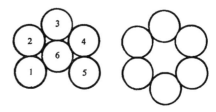

Now this puzzle may be solved in four moves. The more interesting question is: In how many distinct ways can this be done in four moves?

For an analysis of this type of question we imagine the plane covered with circles in the prescribed formation, with six of them covered by discs. The reader may recollect that we did something similar when considering dissections in the last chapter. The discs may be lettered or marked and also the circles in the neighbourhood. We try all possible distinct moves of two discs and select those from which a solution can be completed in two moves. Surprisingly, counting symmetric solutions as distinct, there are 24 distinct solutions. We list these below, where each move in order is given in the notation a—b, c, which means that that move consists in moving disc a till it is in contact with discs b and c.

Solution No.	First Move	Second Move	Third Move	Fourth Move
1	1—2,3	2—6,5	6—1,3	1—6,2
2	1—2,3	4—1,3	3—6,5	5—3,4
3	1—4,5	3—4,1	4—2,6	2—3,4
4	1—4,5	5—2,6	6—4,1	1—6,5
5	2—3,4	3—1,6,5	6—2,4	2—1,6
6	2—3,4	5—2,3	3—1,6	1—3,5
7	2—4,5	5—1,3,6	6—2,4	2—1,6
8	2—4,5	3—2,5	5—1,6	1—5,3
9	3—1,2	5—3,2	2—6,4	4—5,2
10	3—1,2	4—3,1	1—6,5	5—1,4
11	3—1,2	1—2,6,4	6—2,3	3—6,5
12	3—1,2	2—1,6,5	6—3,1	3—6,4
13	3—4,5	2—3,5	5—1,6	1—2,5
14	3—4,5	1—3,4	4—2,6	2—1,4
15	3—4,5	4—1,6,5	6—5,3	3—2,6
16	3—4,5	5—2,6,4	6—3,4	3—1,6
17	4—3,2	3—1,6,5	6—2,4	4—5,6
18	4—3,2	1—4,3	3—5,6	5—3,1
19	4—1,2	1—3,6,5	6—2,4	4—6,5
20	4—1,2	3—1,4	1—6,5	5—1,3
21	5—3,4	4—1,6	6—3,5	5—6,4

Solution No.	First Move	Second Move	Third Move	Fourth Move
22	5—3,4	2—3,5	3—1,6	1—2,3
23	5—1,2	3—2,5	2—6,4	4—3,2
24	5—1,2	1—4,6	6—2,5	5—1,6

It may be noted that there are five types of solution.

Bull's-eye

The writer can think of no better game for youngsters (of any age) aimed to develop the faculty of visualization and spatial judgment than the Bull's-Eye game he played as a child with other youngsters. It is played by two people.

We give a modified version here. At the dictate of player B, A draws a line from X (Home) to whatever number is designated by B and draws a bull's-eye round that. Then, starting from that bull's-eye, he proceeds to the next number to which he is directed and draws a bull's-eye round that. This is continued till A has in turn visited all the fifteen numbers, when he must return Home (to X). The object, for A, is to complete the transit without crossing or touching any number, bull's-eye or path on the way, other than the number he is directed to in each move. The game is played alternately, the one with the most successful complete transits winning. Incidentally, some fascinating designs often crop up in this way.

X	1	2	3
4	5	6	7
8	9	10	11
12	13	14	15

Exercises

1. This represents a train of three cars and a locomotive L. The switch S permits the reversal of either the locomotive or a single car. The problem is to reverse the entire train, keeping the locomotive and cars in the same order, but each reversed.

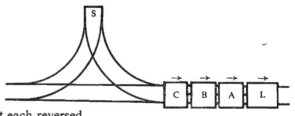

2. The weather is remarkably windless. Two aeroplanes race from New York to Chicago over the same route, one a mile up, the other two miles up. They manoeuvre till both come overhead at the starting point, then start. It turns out they both average the same air speed. Is there any reason to expect one to come in ahead of the other?

3. This represents a tile design for a floor. If approximately 150000 hexagons were used, about how many triangles were required? (Cf. Exs. 106 and 107, Ch. VIII.)

4. This represents a ceiling design of inlaid brass strips with brads at the joins. What is the proportion between the number of strips and brads?

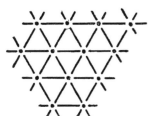

5. As in Ex. 4, what is the approximate proportion between the brads and the strips?

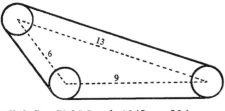

6. Can the full moon ever rise at midnight?
7. Can the moon be eclipsed when half full?
8. Only half of Jupiter is lit up by the sun at any time. Can we (with a telescope) see that planet half full?

9. This represents a pulley arrangement with a belt stretched taut round three pulleys each 2′ in diameter. The distances between the centres are 6′, 9′ and 13′. How long is the belt? (This should be done 'mentally'. See SM March 1949, p. 93.)

10. This represents two equal squares of zinc. How may they be folded together so as to enclose completely a solid volume without any projecting pieces of zinc?

11. What is the greatest number of separate spaces that may be formed by the overlapping of a circle, an oblong and a square?

12. These represent a number of balls that were painted and piled up in a pyramid. Later, on being separated, each ball had a spot for every point of contact. How many spots were there, all told?

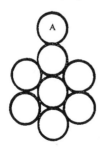

13. This represents equal circles of which all but A remain rigidly fixed. Circle A rolls without slipping till it reaches the next circle. It rolls about that till it reaches the following circle, etc., till it gets back to its initial position at A. By then, how many revolutions about its own axis have been made by the rolling circle? (SM March-June 1950, p. 72.)

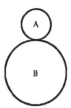

14. Circle A has the diameter a and Circle B the diameter b. Here $a < b$. B is fixed and A rolls about it without slipping till it gets back to its initial position. By then, how many revolutions has A made about its own axis?

15. In Ex. 14, suppose A is fixed and B rolls about it. How many revolutions does B make by the time it returns to its initial position?

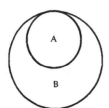

16. Suppose A is within B. Suppose B is rigid and A rolls within it till it returns to its initial position. By then how many revolutions has A made about its own axis?

17. In Ex. 16, suppose A its fixed and B swivels about it till it gets back to its initial position. By then how many revolutions has B made about its own axis?

18. There is an oval track a half mile round. Two motorcycles each with a side car and a passenger start at a point X and travel in opposite directions. One goes steadily at 30 miles per hour, the other at 35 miles per hour. Every time they approach each other each passenger snaps a picture of the other. The final picture is taken as they simultaneously approach X. By then how many pictures has each taken? Note: It may be noted that the distance round the track is irrelevant and that only the ratio of the speeds matters.

19. A cabinet-maker made himself a regular tetrahedron (triangular pyramid) some 2 feet high. He noted there were four faces and six edges. Of the latter each connected with four others. The sixth edge may be considered to be opposite the first. Thus he noted three pairs of opposite edges. One day he divided the figure accurately in half by cutting straight across one edge at its middle and right through the opposite edge along its entire length. Then he carefully glued the two pieces together again. Another day he cut across another edge at its mid-point, then glued the two pieces together again. He did this six times in all, in each case cutting directly across an edge at its middle point. Finally he felt curious as to how many pieces he had glued together. Unable to figure it out, he got a large cauldron, boiled the figure till the pieces separated, then simply counted them. Now can you say just how many pieces he had without going through all that? (SM March-June, 1954 p. 142.)

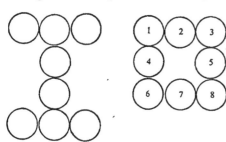

20. Under the same rules as the six disc problem, discussed earlier in the text, change the first configuration into the second in five moves.

There are, essentially, two solutions.

(SM Dec. 1953 p. 242.)

21. In Ex. 20, change back to the first configuration in seven moves.
Note: If, for example, the move 7—3,5 is made, the move 1—6,8 is not permissible unless there is a disc within to delimit the motion of the moved disc.

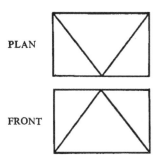

PLAN

FRONT

22. A foundry received as specifications for a solid piece of brass the adjoining PLAN and FRONT projections. It was understood that all the faces were plane. What could be the shape of the object? Show a possible end view and also one in perspective.

161

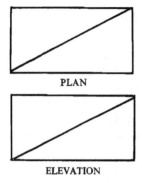

PLAN

ELEVATION

23. The foundry also received these specifications for a part in an experimental machine. The surfaces were to be composed of planes. The foreman was quite excited, saying a number of different shapes would conform, so they telegraphed for instructions. However, the man placing the order was in a hurry to leave on an extended trip and said: "Just use the least material and you'll be all right!" Now suppose you were in the foreman's place. What would you do?

X   NUMERICAL METHODS OF ANALYSIS

One fascinating recreation is the finding of solutions by elementary means for problems usually requiring the application of more technical mathematics. The student of the latter subject often fails to realize just how potent 'elementary' mathematics can be if properly applied. In this chapter we shall concern ourselves with purely arithmetical solutions of certain types of problem without the use of algebraic symbols. We shall, in fact, assume that the reader knows no algebra at all but does understand arithmetic. In this connection, the author has encountered men and women of intelligence who have not had the advantages of an academic education, and who are scared out of their usual wits by the word 'algebra'. For such people, the writer has had to evolve some system that would clarify the solutions of certain problems for them. This chapter contains an explanation of that system. The author is conscious, however, that it would be easier to learn the customary algebraic procedure than to master the technique of this chapter! This will require close attention. However, its application to the more usual, simple cases can be learned readily.

How much of the procedure explained is really new the writer is not in a position to say. That is left to the judgment of the specialist in the history of mathematics.

A simple problem

We shall illustrate the nature of the method by considering a specific problem:

The ages of Father and John now total 91 between them. Father is now three times as old as John was at the time when Father was twice as old as John is now. How old is Father now?

First solution

Before applying our systematic method, let us see what we would be inclined to do with such a problem in the absence of such a method. We cast about for some more or less ingenious analysis that we hope will apply to the particular problem. For another problem we endeavour to hunt up another method. For our present purpose, we may proceed as follows: Suppose we indicate the duration of each age by a line, thus:

A		E		F	B
		:		:	:
		:		:	:
C				G	D

Here AB represents Father's age now, CD represents John's age now, and AE represents Father's age when John was born.

According to the problem, Father is now three times as old as John was a certain time ago. Let G mark John's age at that time. Clearly, since then each has grown older by the same number of years, which is represented by either the line FB or the line GD. From the statement of the problem then, AB must be three times as long as CG. The problem also states that AF, which represents Father's age at that time, must be twice as long as CD, John's present age.

Let us recapitulate:

1. AF is twice as long as CD.

2. AB is three times as long as CG.

Statement 1 may be restated thus:

3. AF is twice the length CG plus twice the length GD. Now if here we add FB to AF this statement requires that, since the lengths FB and GD are equal:

4. AB is twice the length CG plus three times the length GD. Now comparing this with Statement 2, we see that twice the length CG plus twice the length GD must be the same as three times the length of CG. It follows then that three times the length of GD is equal to the length CG.

Now AB is three times CG. Hence AB is nine times GD. Also, CD is four times GD. Hence AB plus CD is thirteen times the length GD. But AB plus CD represents the combined ages of Father and John, which is 91 years. Hence GD is one-thirteenth of this, or 7 years. In other words, the time referred to is 7 years ago.

But AB is nine times GD and CD is four times GD. Hence AB is 63 and CD is 28. That is, Father is 63 years old.

This is well and good. But a similar problem might involve apples and pears, or even ages in a different setting, and the method above might not be effectual. What we should desire is a universal method that would be applicable to *all* problems of this type. We shall apply such a method to the same problem and then discuss those features of it which make it more generally applicable. The following method is purely arithmetical:

Systematic solution

In applying this method, we shall assume a certain figure, presumably in-

164

correct, for Father's age. This will lead to a discrepancy, according to the conditions of our problem. We shall then ascertain by how much we must modify our original assumption for Father's age so as to remove this discrepancy entirely. We proceed then (for the moment we ask the reader to disregard the figures in the small circles):

$$91$$

1. Assume Father is 57 years old. $57 \ (+1)$

2. Subtracting from 91, John's age is found: $34 \ (-1)$

3. One-third of Father's age gives John's age at the time referred to: $3 \ ) \ 57 \ (+1)$

    $19 \ (+\tfrac{1}{3})$

    $34 \ (-1)$

4. Subtracting this from John's age gives the number of years since: $19 \ (+\tfrac{1}{3})$

    $15 \ (-\tfrac{1}{3})$

    $57 \ (+1)$

5. Subtracting this from Father's present age gives his age at the time referred to: $15 \ (-\tfrac{1}{3})$

    $42 \ (+\tfrac{1}{3})$

    $2 \ ) \ 42 \ (+\tfrac{1}{3})$

6. John's present age must be half of that: $21 \ (+\tfrac{1}{6})$

7. But Statement 2 requires John's present age to be 34, if our original assumption for Father's age $34 \ (-1)$

is correct. Subtracting, $21 \ (+\tfrac{1}{6})$

we get the amount of the discrepancy: $13 \ (-1\tfrac{1}{6})$

We ask then: By how much must we alter Father's assumed age of 57 years so that this discrepancy will disappear? This we proceed to ascertain:

Now, whatever we may have assumed Father's age to be, suppose we trace the effect on the discrepancy of an increase by 1 in this assumed age. We shall trace the effect on all the figures we have obtained, by means of the figures shown in the small circles. This supposed increase by 1 is shown by the +1 in the circle adjoining Father's assumed age. Clearly, we obtained the 34 by subtracting from 91. If the subtrahend is now increased by 1, then the remainder must be decreased by 1. This is indicated by the −1 in the circle adjoining the 34. In the next, it is clear that if the 57 is increased by 1, one-third of it must be increased by $\tfrac{1}{3}$, as indicated. Next, we obtained the number 15 by subtracting the 19 from the 34. But we have seen that the 19 would have to be increased by $\frac{1}{3}$, and the 34 decreased by 1. The difference would then have to be less by $1+\frac{1}{3}$, or $\frac{4}{3}$, as shown. Again, the 42 was obtained by subtracting the 15 from the 57. But if the 57 is increased by 1, we have seen that the 15 must be reduced by $\frac{4}{3}$. The remainder would then be increased by the sum of these changes, or $\frac{7}{3}$, as shown. Also, half of this would then be increased by $\frac{7}{6}$, as indicated. Finally, the discrepancy we obtained by subtracting the 21 from the 34. If the subtrahend is increased by $\frac{7}{6}$, and the minuend decreased by 1, the difference would be decreased by $\frac{13}{6}$, as indicated. It must be recognized, also, that this reduction in the discrepancy results from every increase by 1 in the assumed age for Father, *whatever that may have been*. Hence, we add as many 1's to Father's assumed age as $\frac{13}{6}$ is contained in the discrepancy 13. But this is 6. Hence if we add 6 to Father's assumed age the entire discrepancy disappears and we have a correct solution to our problem. Father's age is then $57+6$, or 63 years. John's age is then 28 years.

Discussion of method

It should be noted here that we are asked to determine simultaneously *two* ages, that of Father and John, neither of which is directly specified. Compare this with the following problem:

> If Mr. A used $\frac{1}{3}$ of his present capital to pay debts, and collects $600, he will have $1800 less than twice his original capital. What was his original capital?

Obviously, if Mr. A did not collect any money, he should have $2400 less than twice his original capital. In other words, $\frac{2}{3}$ of his original capital, plus the $2400, is equivalent to twice his original capital. Clearly, then, the $2400 must represent $\frac{4}{3}$ of his original capital, which must then have been $1800.

Now, how does this problem differ from the former? True, we need determine only one figure to solve the problem, whereas in the other we need to find two. Let us examine that problem: We note that *two* independent numerical statements about the ages are given us. The first is that the sum of the ages must be 91 years. Initially, the two ages may each be almost anything between natural limits. Not any pair of ages has this sum. However, there are endless pairs of ages, including fractional ones, which total 91 years. However, the problem asks: Of all possible pairs of ages which total 91 years, which pair conforms to the second condition of the problem? Further, it must be noted that the second condition must not be irrelevant, nor involve the first indirectly. For example, if instead of the second condition we are told that Father's exceeds Uncle Henry's age by as much as Uncle Henry's exceeds John's age, we are not given any new relevant information. The last statement means merely that Uncle Henry's age is half the sum of the other two, and must be $45\frac{1}{2}$ years. It gives us no new information about the two ages required, which, so far, may be any two totalling 91 years. In fact, there may even be a contradiction, if we are told that Henry's age must be, say, 50 years. Suppose, now, our problem requires us to find simultaneously *three* figures, which, apart from the requirements of the problem, may be any three numbers, each from a certain range of possibilities. We have seen that two quantitative statements are sufficient to determine the values of two unknown figures (if we only knew how to find them). So, if another unspecified figure is referred to as an integral part of the problem, we clearly do not have sufficient information to specify all three. The point is, an *additional* quantitative statement about the figures to be determined must be given before we can undertake to ascertain what the figures must be which conform to the requirements. The principle should be clear; that we need three definite quantitative statements to enable us to determine three unknown quantities, four statements to determine four unknown quantities, etc.

To illustrate more definitely, suppose that we are to find, say, the ages of three people. Suppose two statements were given. We have already learned that these would generally determine the values of two unknown figures. Suppose now we arbitrarily assume a value for one of the three ages at random. Then the two statements given us will determine the other two ages that must be associated with this assumed age for one of the three. Assuming another value instead of our original one, we again compute values for the other two ages that must be associated with this assumed age. Of all such triads of ages that we may obtain in this way, which set is correct? So far, *all are*, unless a further condition is implied. We then ask: Out of all the infinitude of associated triads that result from considering only the two statements, which will satisfy a specified third condition? From the first two conditions only we may not as yet know how to sort out that triad of figures from amongst all those possible, but it should begin to be clear now why, for definiteness, another condition must be given, and how it may turn out to be sufficient for the definite determination of the three values required.*

Two other features of this type of problem must be made clear. Suppose we take the problem:

We have two numbers. The first exceeds three times the second by 8. Further, the smaller is 4 less than half the difference between the two numbers. What are the two numbers?

* Carrying on this idea another step, we may realize that, to determine three unknown figures, a fourth quantitative statement may in fact be contradictory.

Consider the second statement. It amounts to saying that half the difference is 4 more than the smaller number. The whole difference is then 8 more than twice the smaller number. The larger number is then 8 more than three times the smaller number. But that is exactly what the first statement requires! We see here, then, that the second statement is merely a disguised form of the first, and tells us nothing new about the numbers in question. It is *redundant*. In fact, it might even result in a contradiction if the statement required the lesser to be, say, 5 less than half the difference between the two numbers! In this case, to enable us to solve the problem definitely, we need another *independent* quantitative statement about the two numbers.

The other item is illustrated in the following problem:

Carl's weight added to Dirk's is 290 lbs. But twice Carl's added to three times Dirk's is 740 lbs. What does each weigh?

Clearly, the second statement is equivalent to saying that Dirk weighs 160 lbs. Thus one of the statements of a problem may in simplified form give the amount of one of the figures required in the problem. Consider what we did in the Father and John age problem. We have two statements, the first simple, the second complex. We retained the first statement and replaced the second by the simplest form of a second statement, namely, that Father is 57 years old. Of course, since we did not guess right (nor did we wish to!), this resulted in a discrepancy when compared with the actual second statement, but the procedure was simplified in that we proceeded *as if we knew* the value of the unknown figure in question, viz., Father's age. We were then enabled to compute simply several figures in order: John's age, the number of years back to the time referred to, the discrepancy, the effect on the discrepancy of every change by 1 in the initial assumed figure and, finally, by how much to alter our assumed figure so as to eliminate this discrepancy and give a correct solution to our actual problem.

Other points of application

It should be noted that the method we have outlined may be applied to a problem in more than one way. For example, referring to the same problem, the computation might have been as follows:

	Father's Age	John's Age
Now	57 $(+1)$	34 (-1)
Earlier	68 (-2)	19 $(+1)$

Number of Years Back	$11 \left(-3\right)$	$15 \left(-\frac{1}{3}\right)$
LATER*		
Discrepancy between the last two figures:		$26 \left(-\frac{10}{3}\right)$

Here the 34 was obtained as before by subtracting the assumed value 57 from the sum 91. The 19 is one-third of the 57, according to the problem, and the 68 is twice the 34. Subtracting the 19 from the figure 34 gives the number of years ago. But the same number should have been obtained by a similar subtraction in Father's column. It would have been if our original guess as to Father's age were correct. But there is a discrepancy of 26 between the last two numbers. As before, the figures in the small circles trace the effect on each of the figures, computed in order, of an increase by 1 in the assumed age for Father. We observe that the net reduction in our discrepancy is $\frac{13}{3}$. We add as many 1's to Father's assumed age as $\frac{13}{3}$ goes into the discrepancy, 26, getting 6, as before, for the desired modification. It should be noted that, despite this lengthy expository presentation, an actual solution of such a problem can be found quickly by a few compact simple computations. It should also be noted that this and other similar problems may be solved by assuming initially some value for an incidental, but vital, figure in the problem; as, in this case, the number of years elapsed between the two times in question. We shall presently illustrate that in a more complex problem. We emphasize again that it is not necessary to go through all the formal statements made in this solution in applying it to a similar problem. A few figures, generally without other writing, in compact form, are all that is necessary. In age problems, representing various ages by lines of corresponding lengths, and placing all figures computed along such lines, is very convenient.

Another problem

We shall try out our method on a problem which appeared some years ago, of which we do not know the origin:

> I A piece of rope weighs four ounces per foot. It is passed over a pulley and on one end is suspended a weight and on the other a monkey. The whole system is in equilibrium.

* In Father's column we have to subtract a larger from a smaller number. We can obviate that in either of two ways: 1) By assuming a different value for Father's age now. 2) By keeping Father's age as assumed, but slightly altering the sequence of the computation. For example, having obtained the 15 from the second column, we add that to the figure 68 in the first column to give Father's age now. This yields 83, which shows a discrepancy from Father's assumed age, 57, of 26 years. We now proceed as before.

II The weight of the monkey in pounds equals the age of the monkey's mother in years, and the age of the monkey's mother added to the age of the monkey is four years. The monkey's mother is (A) twice as old now as the monkey was (B) when the mother was one-half as old as the monkey will be when (C) the monkey is three times as old as the monkey's mother was when (D) the monkey's mother was three times as old as the monkey.

III The weight of the rope or the weight at the end of the rope is one-half as much again as the difference in weight between the weight and the weight plus the weight of the monkey.

IV How long is the rope?

For convenient reference, we have numbered the paragraphs and put letters at each mention of a different time in Paragraph II. From Paragraph III we need the weight of the monkey. This is known if, according to the first sentence of Paragraph II, we know the age of the monkey's mother. The rest of paragraph II is concerned with ascertaining the ages of the monkey and its mother.

There are two statements concerning the ages in question. The first, as part of the first sentence in Paragraph II, tells us that the ages of both monkeys total 4 years. The complicated second sentence of this paragraph gives us the only other information regarding the relative ages we are to find. But this, as we have seen in our earlier discussion, together with the statement as to the sum of the ages, should be sufficient to specify them definitely, if we can analyze the requirement. This we now proceed to do. To avoid fractions as far as possible, we shall take smaller time units for the ages. We could take tenths of a year, but, since months are already established, they will be just as convenient. The sum of both ages is then 48 months. We shall assume the mother to be 28 months old now. This will require the monkey to be 20 months old now. We shall note what discrepancy results from testing our assumption with the second statement of Paragraph II; we shall then find what difference in this discrepancy results from an increase by 1 month in the assumed age of the mother, and shall increase this assumed age by as many months as would reduce this discrepancy to nothing.

We carry through the following computation: (For the present, we disregard the numbers in circles.)

Total of both ages   48

Assumed age for mother   28 (+1)

Monkey's present age   20 (-1)

170

Half the mother's present age, or the monkey's age	2) 28	(+1)
at B is	14	$(+\frac{1}{2})$
Monkey's present age	20	(−1)
Monkey's age at B	14	$(+\frac{1}{2})$
Number of months back to B	6	$(-\frac{3}{2})$
Mother's age now	28	(+1)
Number of months back to B	6	$(-\frac{3}{2})$
Mother's age at B	22	$(+\frac{5}{2})$
	2	
Monkey's age at C	44	(+5)
	3) 44	(+5)
Mother's age at D	$14\frac{2}{3}$	$(+\frac{5}{3})$
Mother's present age	28	(+1)
Mother's age at D	$14\frac{2}{3}$	$(+\frac{5}{3})$
Number of months back to D	$13\frac{1}{3}$	$(-\frac{2}{3})$
Monkey's present age	20	(−1)
Number of months back to D	$13\frac{1}{3}$	$(-\frac{2}{3})$
Monkey's age at D	$6\frac{2}{3}$	$(-\frac{1}{3})$
	3	
Three times monkey's age at D	20	(−1)
Mother's age at D	$14\frac{2}{3}$	$(+\frac{5}{3})$
Discrepancy	$5\frac{1}{3}$	$(-\frac{8}{3})$

We now follow through the result of an increase by 1 month in the assumed age of the mother, *whatever that assumed age may be.* This effect we shall trace by the numbers in the small circles. We shall note that these resulting changes in the figures of our computation do not depend upon the actual figures we have so far had to use, but *only on the way they have been obtained*, according to the conditions of the problem. To begin with, whatever we may first have assumed, suppose the mother's age were assumed to be 1 month greater. The method of computation shows that the monkey's age would have to be just 1 month less. Half of mother's age, or the monkey's age at B, would be $\frac{1}{2}$ month more. The number of months back to B would then be reduced by $\frac{3}{2}$. The next computation shows that the mother's age at B would have to be $\frac{5}{2}$ months greater. From this, the mother's age at C would be 5 months greater. The next step shows that the mother's age at D would be increased by $\frac{5}{3}$. The next computation shows that the number of months back to D would be reduced by $\frac{4}{3}$. Tracing this modification to the next step, the monkey's age at D would be $\frac{1}{3}$ month less. Three times this age would then be 1 month less, as shown. The discrepancy was obtained by the last subtraction. But as a result of our assumption of an increase by 1 in the mother's age, the minuend would be reduced by 1 and the subtrahend increased by $\frac{5}{3}$. The difference, which is the discrepancy, would then be reduced by $\frac{8}{3}$. Further, this reduction results from an increase by 1 in the assumed age of the mother. Clearly, then, we add as many 1's to this assumed age, *whatever it may be*, as the reduction $\frac{8}{3}$ goes into the entire discrepancy. The discrepancy here is $5\frac{1}{3}$, or $\frac{16}{3}$. $\frac{16}{3}$ divided by $\frac{8}{3}$ is 2. Hence, to eliminate this entire discrepancy exactly, we add 2 to the assumed age for the mother.*

Therefore the correct age for the mother is 30 months, or $2\frac{1}{2}$ years. The correct age for the monkey is then 18 months, or $1\frac{1}{2}$ years.

From the final sentence of Paragraph II, the weight of the monkey is $2\frac{1}{4}$ lbs.

From Paragraph III, the difference in weight between the weight on one end of the rope and the weight plus the weight of the monkey is simply the weight of the monkey, or $2\frac{1}{4}$ lbs. The weight of the rope is then one and one-half times this, or $\frac{15}{4}$ lbs. Since each foot of the rope weighs 4 oz., or $\frac{1}{4}$ lb., the length of the rope is clearly 15 ft.

Apparent failure of the method

In applying this method, it must be understood clearly that an increase by 1 in an assumed value results in a definite change in another value, *whatever that other value may be*. Otherwise no logical conclusion may be drawn and the method fails. For example, let us take the following problem:

> In travelling a mile, the front wheels of a wagon make 110 revolutions more than the rear wheels. If the front wheels had a diameter one-sixth less, and the rear wheels one-quarter less, the front wheels would make 88 revolutions more than the rear wheels in travelling the same distance. What are the circumferences of the wheels?

* If this increase by 1 in the assumed value for the mother's age resulted in an *increase* in the discrepancy, we would *reduce* the assumed age by the amount obtained by our division.

As usual, let us replace one of these complex statements, say the second, by the assumption that the front wheel has a circumference of 8 ft. Then it would make $\frac{5280}{8}$, or 660 revolutions in a mile. We proceed as follows:

Revolutions of front wheels	660
Difference	110
Revolutions of rear wheels	550

The circumference of a rear wheel is then $\frac{5280}{550}$, or $\frac{48}{5}$ ft. But from the second condition, the wheels would be of circumferences $\frac{20}{3}$ and $\frac{36}{5}$ ft., respectively. The revolutions to the mile would then be:

Front wheels	792
Rear wheels	$733\frac{1}{3}$
Difference	$58\frac{2}{3}$
Required difference	88
Discrepancy	$29\frac{1}{3}$

Now suppose the circumference of the smaller wheel were 1 ft. greater, that is, 9 ft. The number of revolutions it would make in a mile would then be $\frac{5280}{9}$, or $586\frac{2}{3}$. We proceed to compare this with the former number, 660, but then realize that the difference depends upon the particular values we used for the circumference; we cannot assign a definite uniform increase or decrease in the number of revolutions per mile to each foot of increase in the circumference of the wheel, *regardless of what that circumference might be*. Only on such an assumption can our method be applied. But in this case we get a *different* decrease in the number of revolutions per mile for each increase of 1 ft. in the circumference of the wheel, *for each size of the wheel*. Does this mean that our method is not applicable to this type of problem? The answer is 'No, it *is* applicable'—we must simply apply it differently. The solution follows:

. Instead of focusing our attention on the circumference of a wheel, let us consider rather the number of revolutions per mile made by that wheel. If we please, we may again choose 660 as the number of revolutions per mile of the smaller wheel. The analysis is quite simple now. If the front wheel makes 660 revolutions, then by the problem the rear wheel makes 110 less, or 550 revolutions per mile. Now, whatever the size of the wheel, if it is reduced to $\frac{5}{6}$ of its original diameter, it will make $\frac{6}{5}$ as many revolutions over the same distance. But $\frac{6}{5}$ of 660 is 792. Similarly, the rear wheel would make $\frac{4}{3}$ as many revolutions, if its diameter be reduced to $\frac{3}{4}$ of its original size. The rear wheel would then make $733\frac{1}{3}$ revolutions. The difference is $58\frac{2}{3}$, whereas the problem requires 88, yielding a discrepancy of $29\frac{1}{3}$. The computation thus far is conveniently represented in the following scheme, where, for the moment, we disregard the figures in circles:

660 $(+1)$	550 $(+1)$	
792 $(+\frac{8}{5})$	$733\frac{1}{3}$ $(+\frac{4}{3})$	
Difference	$58\frac{2}{3}$ $(-\frac{2}{15})$	
Required difference	88	
Discrepancy	$29\frac{1}{3}$ $(+\frac{2}{15})$	

Now suppose the number 660 be increased by 1. Then the number 550 must also be increased by 1, since the difference must remain 110. Further, *whatever the size of the wheel, or the distance covered,* for every additional revolution it makes on one basis it now makes $\frac{8}{5}$ revolutions on the modified basis. Similarly for the rear wheel: for every additional revolution it makes under the first condition it now makes $\frac{4}{3}$ revolutions, regardless of its size. The difference is then modified by $\frac{2}{15}$ for every increase by 1 in the figure 660. We then *reduce* the 660 by as many 1's as $\frac{2}{15}$ goes into $29\frac{1}{3}$, or 220. Hence the front wheel makes 440 revolutions per mile and the rear wheel 330. The circumference of the front wheel is then $\frac{5280}{440}$, or 12 ft.; that of the rear wheel is then $\frac{5280}{330}$, or 16 ft.

Extended application of the method

We now apply our method to the finding simultaneously of *three* quantities. Consider the problem:

> A manufacturing jeweller wished to buy 100 lbs. of a certain alloy composed of gold, silver and copper. He was to be charged at the rate of $300 a lb. for the gold, $20 a lb. for the silver, and $.25 a lb. for the copper. He was offered a sample of such of alloy at the average price of $36.15 per lb. This was not satisfactory. However, he did purchase 100 lbs. of alloy containing one-tenth less silver and one-half as much gold at the average price of $20.57 per lb. How many lbs. of each metal did the alloy contain?

We shall follow the principle we adopted for the simpler type of problem. We have to ascertain three weights. We shall arbitrarily assume a tentative value for one of them, disregarding for the moment one of the conditions of the problem. As we have seen, this is tantamount to replacing one of the statements of the problem by another in the simplest possible form. Having thus disregarded one of the statements of the problem, and

174

'knowing' the numerical value of one of the weights, the remaining conditions of the problem will enable us by the method already explained to find the other two weights. This we do in the manner shown. We thus obtain values for the other two weights which must result if our original 'guess' were correct. But we now compare our findings with the requirements of the statement we have tentatively disregarded. This leads to a new discrepancy. We then review our first computation, which in itself involves the consideration and elimination of a discrepancy, and trace the effect on the figures thus obtained of an increase by 1 in the assumed weight. This enables us to ascertain at once by how much to alter this first assumption for one of the weights to eliminate entirely the final discrepancy, and so give us a set of correct answers. There are thus two vital steps to our solution:

First, we shall assume that the metal bought contained exactly 3 lbs. of gold. To begin with we perform the following computation, where for the moment we disregard the figures in rectangles:

Total weight of metal in lbs.	100	
Weight of gold	3	+1
Weight of silver and copper in lbs.	97	−1
Total cost in dollars	2057	
Cost of the gold	900	+300
Cost of silver and copper combined	1157	−300

We thus have a preliminary problem to solve. This may be put as follows:

> 97 lbs. of an alloy of silver and copper are purchased for $1157. The silver in it cost $20 per lb., the copper $.25 per lb. How much of each metal was purchased?

This subsidiary problem we know how to solve. We do so in the following computation, where we again disregard the figures in circles or rectangles:

We shall suppose that there were, say, 20 lbs. of silver in this alloy. We shall then see by how much to modify this assumption so as to satisfy the requirements of the subsidiary problem. Then we shall examine the whole computation to see how it must be modified so as to satisfy the neglected conditions of our original problem. We have then:

175

Total weight in lbs. of silver and copper	$\underline{97}$	$\boxed{-1}$
Assumed weight of silver	$20\ \textcircled{+1}$	
Weight of copper	$77\ \textcircled{-1}$	$\boxed{-1}$
Value of silver at \$20 per lb.	$400\ \textcircled{+20}$	
Value of copper at \$.25 per lb.	$19\tfrac{1}{4}\ \textcircled{$-\frac{1}{4}$}$	$\boxed{-\frac{1}{4}}$
Cost of silver and copper together	$419\tfrac{1}{4}\ \textcircled{$+\frac{79}{4}$}$	$\boxed{-\frac{1}{4}}$
Required cost	1157	$\boxed{-300}$
Discrepancy	$737\tfrac{3}{4}\ \textcircled{$-\frac{79}{4}$}$	$\boxed{-\frac{1199}{4}}$

$$\boxed{-\tfrac{1199}{4}}$$

Correction $\qquad 737\tfrac{3}{4}\ \div\ \tfrac{79}{4}\ =\ \tfrac{2951}{79}\boxed{-\tfrac{1199}{79}}$

$$\boxed{-\tfrac{1199}{79}}$$

Correct weight of silver $\qquad 20\ +\ \tfrac{2951}{79}\ =\ \tfrac{4531}{79}\boxed{-\tfrac{1199}{79}}$

$$\boxed{-1}\qquad\boxed{-\tfrac{1199}{79}}$$

Correct weight of copper $\qquad 77\ -\ \tfrac{2951}{79}\ =\ \tfrac{3132}{79}\boxed{+\tfrac{1199}{79}}$

The corrections in the silver and copper were obtained in the usual way by tracing the changes in our figures resulting from an increase by 1 in the assumed weight of the silver. This is traced by the figures in circles. What have we now? Merely this; that *if* 3 lbs. of gold were purchased, the silver would have to be $\tfrac{4531}{79}$ lbs. and the copper $\tfrac{3132}{79}$ lbs. For a different assumption as to the weight of gold there would presumably be different figures for the silver and copper. But *the method of computation* would be identical with the procedure in the scheme above. We now trace the effect on each of the figures in this computation of an increase by 1 in the weight assumed *for the gold*. These changes we shall indicate by the numbers in the small rectangles. We recapitulate:

Assumed weight of gold in lbs.	3	$\boxed{+1}$
Resulting computed weight of silver	$\tfrac{4531}{79}$	$\boxed{-\tfrac{1199}{79}}$
Computed weight for copper	$\tfrac{3132}{79}$	$\boxed{+\tfrac{1199}{79}}$

This is on the basis of what the jeweller actually bought. But the first sample offered him contained twice as much gold and $\tfrac{10}{9}$ as much silver. Hence in the sample there were:

Gold in lbs.	6	$+2$
Silver in lbs.	$\frac{45810}{711}$	$-\frac{1100}{711}$
Gold and silver together	$\frac{49576}{711}$	$-\frac{10568}{711}$
Weight of gold, silver and copper	100	
Computed weight of copper in sample	$\frac{21524}{711}$	$+\frac{10568}{711}$
Cost of gold in sample	1800	$+600$
Cost of silver in sample	$\frac{906200}{711}$	$-\frac{239800}{711}$
Cost of copper in sample	$\frac{5381}{711}$	$+\frac{2645}{711}$
Total cost of sample	$3082\frac{1}{9}$	$+266\frac{1}{2}$
Required cost of sample	3615	
Discrepancy	$532\frac{8}{9}$	$-266\frac{1}{2}$

We assume now that we modify our assumption for the weight of the gold by increasing it by 1. This is indicated by the 1 in the small rectangle adjoining the figure 3. We shall trace the effect of this alteration in the weight of the gold on the last discrepancy we have noted. First we reiterate that the method of computing the weights of the other two metals that correspond to this modified value for the weight of the gold remains the same—only the figures change. Further, the incidental changes noted by the figures in circles *are not affected at all*. Let us trace the figures that are affected. To begin with, the figure 97 was obtained by subtracting the 3 from 100. If this 3 is increased by 1, the difference, in this case 97, is decreased by 1. This is shown by the -1 in the rectangle adjoining the 97. Further, whatever the incidental assumption for the weight of the silver may be on subtracting from 97, the residue is decreased by the same amount as the 97; 1 in this instance. Again, proceeding to the following figures, the value of the copper is decreased by $\frac{1}{4}$, as indicated by that figure in the rectangle. The value of the silver and the copper residue is then similarly reduced by $\frac{1}{4}$. We also note that with 1 lb. of gold more, the cost of the silver and copper combined would be $300 less, as shown. The discrepancy in the incidental problem, *whatever it may be,* is then decreased by $\frac{1100}{4}$. Now the correction in the assumed value for the silver in the subsidiary problem was obtained by dividing the discrepancy by $\frac{79}{4}$. But for every increase by 1 in the assumed value for the weight of the gold in the original problem we have seen that the discrepancy would be reduced by $\frac{1100}{4}$. Hence the correction would be reduced by $\frac{1100}{4} \div \frac{79}{4}$, or $\frac{1100}{79}$, as shown in the rectangle. Along with this, the weight of the copper would

177

be increased by a corresponding amount $\frac{1120}{79}$. We thus see how the computed weights for the silver and the copper are altered corresponding to a change of 1 in the assumed weight for the gold. This also enables us to see by how much the value of the entire alloy is altered. We see then that the entire discrepancy, $532\frac{2}{8}$, is reduced by $266\frac{4}{8}$ for every increase by 1 in the assumed weight of the gold. Hence we add as many 1's to this assumed weight as $266\frac{4}{8}$ goes into $532\frac{2}{8}$. But this is 2. Hence the correct weight of the gold in the alloy is 5 lbs. Again, adding twice the correction, $\frac{1120}{79}$, to the computed weight of the copper, the correct weight of the copper becomes 68 lbs. Similarly, reducing the computed weight for the silver, $\frac{4531}{79}$, by twice the correction, $\frac{1199}{79}$, gives the correct value, 27 lbs., for that metal. This solves our problem.

The writer has made no attempt to avoid fractions, since it is a mere accident that the answers come out integral. The point is that, whatever the values of the answers, this method will lead directly to them.

Application to more complex type

In the problems so far considered, each contained one comparatively simple statement, which served as a convenient starting point. But suppose all statements are involved. The method will still apply. Let us consider the following age problem (In this, we have marked with a small letter every reference to a distinct time):

> A is (a) half as old as both A and B together will be (b) when B is 5 years older than both together were when (c) A was half as old as B will be (d) 10 years from now. When A is (e) three times as old as B was (g) when both together were as old as A will be (h) 10 years hence, B will be (e) twice as old as A was (f) 15 years ago. How old is each?

Indeed, this does seem prohibitive and discouraging. Nevertheless, with a little patience, we shall see that the technique we have already developed will serve to solve this type of problem just as readily. Again, we must point out that what may be a simple explanation when given verbally often takes on length and apparent complexity when every detail has to be written out. In actual application very little is written out formally, the computation being simple and compact. However, let us begin the attack:

We shall replace the complex second statement of our problem by the simplest possible kind of statement, that B is now (at a) 40 years old, and solve the simplified problem thus formed first. We proceed as follows, where for the moment we disregard the figures in the small squares:

B's age at a	40 $\boxed{+1}$
	10
B's age at d	$\overline{50}$ $\boxed{+1}$
	2) $\overline{50}$ $\boxed{+1}$
A's age at c	25 $\boxed{+\frac{1}{2}}$

The first statement now becomes involved. It is not apparent what age for A goes with the assumed age for B even if we consider the first statement of our problem only. We wish then to compute the age for A that corresponds to the value 40 for B's age. As usual, we assume some value for this age and then correct it to fit the requirement. Hence:

Assume A's age at a to be	60 $\ominus 1$	
A's age at c	$\underline{25}$	$\boxed{+\frac{1}{2}}$
Years ago to c	35 $\ominus 1$	$\boxed{-\frac{1}{2}}$
B's age at a	$\underline{40}$	$\boxed{+1}$
B's age at c	5 $\oplus 1$	$\boxed{+\frac{1}{2}}$
A's age at c	$\underline{25}$	$\boxed{+\frac{1}{2}}$
Sum of both ages at c	30 $\oplus 1$	$\boxed{+2}$
	5	
B's age at b	$\overline{35}$ $\oplus 1$	$\boxed{+2}$
B's age at a	$\underline{40}$	$\boxed{+1}$
Years back to b	5 $\ominus 1$	$\boxed{-1}$
A's age at a	60 $\ominus 1$	
A's age at b	$\underline{55}$ $\bigcirc 0$	$\boxed{+1}$
B's age at b	35 $\oplus 1$	$\boxed{+2}$
Sum of both ages at b	$\overline{90}$ $\oplus 1$	$\boxed{+3}$
Twice A's age at a	120 $\ominus 2$	
Discrepancy	$\overline{30}$ $\ominus 3$	$\boxed{-3}$

The figures in the circles show the changes in the figures due to a change by 1 in the assumed value for the age of A at a. For every decrease by 1 in this assumed age there is a decrease of 3 in the discrepancy. Hence we decrease the assumed age for A by as many 1's as 3 goes into 30. Hence we have:

179

A's assumed age	60
Correction	10
A's corrected age	50

The computation thus far shows that if we assume B's age at *a* to be 40, and disregard the second statement of our problem, A's age would have to be 50. Further, whatever we would have shown for B's age, the computation would be the same; only some of the figures changing. Further, in any case, the figures in the circles remain the same. Suppose now, that whatever we may have chosen for B's age, we increase it by 1. Let us trace the necessary modifications in our computation by the figures in the small rectangles. These explain themselves if followed through seriatim. These figures show that the effect on the discrepancy is a reduction of 3 for every increase by 1 in B's assumed age. Thus A's age will be reduced by $3 \div 3$, or 1, less than before. That is, A's computed age will be just 1 more. The reasoning shows now that, so far as the first statement of our problem goes, if B is 40 years old, A is 50, and that for every decrease by 1 in B's assumed age there must be a decrease by 1 in A's age. This equality of modification is accidental, and is not general.

We are now prepared to consider the second of our conditions. We suppose that B is 40 years old; hence A must be 50. This pair of ages is presumably incorrect, and will lead to a discrepancy. This we determine as before:

A's age at *a*	50 △
Years back to *f*	15
A's age at *f*	35 △
	2
B's age at *e*	70 △
B's age at *a*	40 △
Years back to *e*	30 △
A's age at *a*	50 △
A's age at *e*	80 △
3) 80 △	
B's age at *g*	$26\frac{2}{3}$ △ .
B's age at *a*	40 △
Years back to *g*	$13\frac{1}{3}$ △

180

A's age at a $\underline{50}$ △

A's age at g $36\frac{2}{3}$ △

B's age at g $\underline{26\frac{2}{3}}$ △

Sum of both ages at g $63\frac{1}{3}$ △

     $\underline{10}$

A's computed age at a $53\frac{1}{3}$ △

A's assumed age at a $\underline{50}$ △

Discrepancy $3\frac{1}{3}$ △

Now we know that for every decrease by 1 in B's assumed age there must be a decrease by 1 in A's assumed age. The figures in the triangles show the effect of these unit decreases on the discrepancy. Hence, to remove this discrepancy, we reduce each of our assumed ages by as many times as $\frac{1}{3}$ goes into the entire discrepancy, $\frac{10}{3}$. But this is 10. Hence the correct ages are 40 for A and 30 for B. This solves our problem.

A more extended problem

We shall conclude this section with a comparatively simple problem involving the determination of four numbers simultaneously. From the data below, we are to determine the cost per unit of each of four items; fountain pens, hats, overcoats, wrist watches.

(1) A pen, 2 hats and 9 overcoats exceed in cost 5 wrist watches by $294.
(2) 7 pens and 11 wrist watches cost more by $123 than 5 hats and 2 overcoats.
(3) The cost of 3 pens, 8 hats, 4 overcoats and 7 watches is $402.
(4) The cost of 16 pens, 13 hats, 5 overcoats and 9 watches is $626.
I   We replace one of these four statements, say (4), by a simple one, namely,
(4') A wrist watch costs $12.

We now set out to solve the problem posed by this and the first three given statements. After having done so, we shall compare the result with the actual statement 4, arrive at a discrepancy, and then proceed to remove that. In the light of (4'), the first three statements become:
(1') 1 pen, 2 hats and 9 overcoats cost $354.
(2') 5 hats and 2 overcoats cost more by $9 than 7 pens.
(3') 3 pens, 8 hats and 4 overcoats cost $318.
We note that these new figures were obtained as follows:

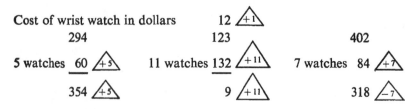

Cost of wrist watch in dollars 12 △+1

294

5 watches 60 △+5

354 △+5

123

11 watches 132 △+11

9 △+11

402

7 watches 84 △+7

318 △−7

For the present we disregard the numbers in the triangles.

We have now an intermediate problem, posed by the three conditions (1'), (2'), (3'). To save possible confusion, suppose that we subcontract the solution of this subsidiary problem to a Mr. A. He, regardless of our use of his solution in the overall problem, may proceed as shown below.

II Replace one of the three conditions, say (3'), by a simpler one, namely, (3″) Let one overcoat cost $10.

In the light of this, the two other conditions become:
(1″) 1 pen and 2 hats cost $264.
(2″) 7 pens cost more than 5 hats by $11.

The new figures are obtained as follows:

1 overcoat   10 $\boxed{+1}$

354   △+5

9 overcoats   90 $\boxed{+9}$

264 $\boxed{-9}$ △+5

9   △+11

2 overcoats 20 $\boxed{+2}$

11 $\boxed{+2}$ △−11

Mr. A now has to solve the incidental problem posed by statements (1″) and (2″). Again, to save confusion, we may suppose Mr. A lets that job out to a subcontractor who may not be interested in the further use of his solution. The latter, Mr. B, may proceed as shown below.

III Replace (2″) by the simple statement,
(2‴) Let each hat cost $50.
Then (1″) becomes,
(1‴) 1 pen costs $164.

The last figure was obtained as follows:

1 hat   50 $\oplus{+1}$

264        $\boxed{-9}$ △+5

2 hats   100 $\oplus{+2}$

1 pen   164 $\ominus{-2}$ $\boxed{-9}$ △+5

Mr. B now compares his figures with statement (2″) which he had momentarily replaced by (2‴) and obtains a discrepancy:

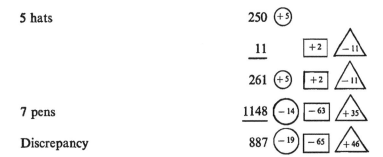

5 hats

7 pens

Discrepancy

Mr. B now traces the effect of a change by 1 in his assumed value for the cost of a hat. This is shown by the figures in the circles. He corrects his assumed value of 50 in dollars for the hat by adding the sum

For the pen he then subtracts,

$$2 \times 46\tfrac{13}{19} = 93\tfrac{7}{19}$$

The new values are then obtained:

50

164

$46\tfrac{13}{19}$

$93\tfrac{7}{19}$

Hat $96\tfrac{13}{19}$

Pen $70\tfrac{12}{19}$

IV   This computation, minus the numbers in the rectangles and triangles, Mr. B turns over to Mr. A. Mr. A notes the rôles played by the figures given Mr. B in statements (1″) and (2″). He traces the effect of a change by 1 in the value assumed for the cost of a coat on Mr. B's determination of the cost of a hat and of a pen. These effects are to be followed through in the numbers in the rectangles. Further, he notes that the changes due to an alteration in the value he assumed do not affect the figures in the circles.

Mr. A knows that, for his subsidiary problem, if he replaces (3′) by assuming that an overcoat costs $10, then corresponding to that assumption, the cost of a hat and the cost of a pen are as indicated above. He now checks these values with statement (3′) and finds a discrepancy:

3 pens	$211\frac{17}{19}$ $\boxed{-\frac{122}{19}}$	$\triangle{+\frac{13}{19}}$
8 hats	$773\frac{9}{19}$ $\boxed{-\frac{520}{19}}$	$\triangle{+\frac{208}{19}}$
4 coats	$\underline{40}$ $\boxed{+4}$	
Sum	$1025\frac{7}{19}$ $\boxed{-\frac{467}{19}}$	$\triangle{+\frac{17}{19}}$
	$\underline{318}$	$\triangle{-7}$
Discrepancy	$707\frac{7}{19}$ $\boxed{-\frac{187}{19}}$	$\triangle{+\frac{810}{19}}$

Mr. A then corrects his assumed value for the cost of an overcoat in dollars by adding,

$$\triangle{+\frac{810}{19}}$$

$$\frac{13440}{19} \div \frac{567}{19} = \frac{13440}{567} = \frac{640}{27} = 23\frac{19}{27} \quad \triangle{+\frac{170}{189}}$$

His corrected figures for the solution of the problem posed by conditions (1′), (2′), (3′) are then obtained as follows:

Assumed cost of overcoat	10	
Correction	$23\frac{19}{27}$	$\triangle{+\frac{170}{189}}$
Corrected cost of overcoat	$33\frac{19}{27}$	$\triangle{+\frac{170}{189}}$
Cost of pen as forwarded by Mr. B	$70\frac{12}{19}$	$\triangle{+\frac{3}{19}}$
Correction applied by Mr. A:		
	$\triangle{+\frac{170}{189}}$	
$\frac{41}{19} \times \frac{640}{27} = 51\frac{77}{513}$	$\triangle{+\frac{6970}{3591}}$	
Mr. A's value for pen	$19\frac{13}{27}$	$\triangle{-\frac{307}{189}}$
Cost of hat from Mr. B	$96\frac{13}{19}$	$\triangle{+\frac{18}{19}}$
Correction by Mr. A:		
$\frac{65}{19} \times \frac{640}{27} = 81\frac{47}{513}$	$\triangle{+\frac{11050}{3591}}$	
Mr. A's value for hat	$15\frac{16}{27}$	$\triangle{-\frac{184}{189}}$

184

V   These figures, minus the numbers in the triangles, are then turned over to us. They represent the cost of each of the other items that follows on our assuming the cost of a wrist watch to be $12 and ignoring condition (4).

We trace the effect of a change of 1 in our assumed value for the cost of a watch. This we follow through by the figures in the triangles. We must observe that no change resulting from this alteration of our assumed value affects the figures within the circles or the squares, since these depend only on the way the computation is carried out, not on the specific values obtained.

Now, the values we have obtained for the cost of the pen, hat and coat were on the supposition that a wrist watch cost $12; this replacing condition (4). We have also the effect of a change of 1 in our assumed number. Now we consider condition (4) to find the discrepancy. Then we can eliminate that as our final step.

Cost of 16 pens	$311\frac{19}{27}$	$-\frac{5892}{189}$
Cost of 13 hats	$202\frac{19}{27}$	$-\frac{1872}{189}$
Cost of 5 overcoats	$168\frac{14}{27}$	$+\frac{880}{189}$
Cost of 9 watches	108	$+9$
Sum	$790\frac{25}{27}$	$-\frac{4453}{189}$
But (4) requires this to be	626	
Discrepancy	$164\frac{25}{27}$	$-\frac{4453}{189}$

Our final correction is then,

$$\tfrac{4453}{27} \div \tfrac{4453}{189} = 7.$$

We now correct our values for a final determination:

Pen	Hat	Overcoat	Wrist Watch
$19\frac{13}{27}$	$15\frac{16}{27}$	$33\frac{19}{27}$	12
$-12\frac{13}{27}$	$-4\frac{16}{27}$	$+6\frac{8}{27}$	$+7$
7	11	40	19

Whole number problems

We have seen that, when two numerical quantities are to be determined, two independent conditions are required. If we restrict ourselves to one of such a pair of statements about two quantities, we know that for every choice of a value for either of the two numbers in question we may compute a corresponding value for the other. Thus each quantitative statement establishes an indefinite number of pairs of numbers which conform to the requirement of the quantitative condition. However, a number of problems imply another condition. For example, suppose the problem dealt with the number of men and the number of women in a room. In this case, if we consider a single quantitative statement, we may get an indefinite multiplicity of pairs of numbers that conform to the numerical requirement. But the tacit requirement is that all the number pairs must be of whole numbers. Thus not every number pair will do. In fact, generally, only certain definite pairs will do—sometimes only one pair, and sometimes not even one! This gives rise to a class of problem where the number of numerical requirements is less than the number of numbers we are to determine, and where all the numbers to be found must be integral. We shall consider one or two types.

A typical problem

For this purpose, let us first take up the following problem:

> A certain business man was out of funds, and cashed at the bank a cheque he had received for an odd amount. After spending $2.10 he was surprised to note that he had left twice as much money as called for by the face value of the cheque. He then noted that the bank teller had made the mistake of giving him dollars for cents, and vice versa. What was the amount of the cheque?*

Now we have to consider two numbers, the number of dollars, and the number of cents. The cheque called for a sum of money which was, in cents, 100 times the first number plus the second. What the man received was, in cents, 100 times the second number plus the first. Let us compare the following sums:

I   100 times the second number plus the first number.
II   Twice 100 times the first number plus twice the second number plus 210.
According to the statement of our problem these two sums must be equal. If we omit the first number from sum I we must omit an equal amount from sum II. Thus:
Ia   100 times the second number.
IIa   199 times the first number plus twice the second number plus 210.
These sums must be equal. If we now omit twice the second number from the sum IIa we must also omit it from sum Ia, to have the residues still equal. The result takes the form: 98 times the second number is equal to 199 times the first number increased by 210.

* In Ch. IV this problem was considered from a different viewpoint.

186

Of course, if we knew either of the two figures, we could at once compute the other. In fact, as we have seen, for any choice of either number we may compute a definite value for the other. The trouble here is that not every choice will do, for the computed values may be fractional. Let us assume the dollars figure to be 20. Then 98 times the second, or cents number, is equal to 199 times 20 plus 210. We thus carry out the following computation:

$$
\begin{array}{r}
\overset{+1}{} \\
20 \times 199 = 3980 \;\;_{+199} \\
210 \\
\hline
4190 \;\;_{+199} \\
42 \\
\hline
98\,)\,\overline{4190} \;\;_{+199} \\
392 \\
\hline
270 \\
196 \\
\hline
74 \;\;_{+199} \text{ or } _{+3}\,,
\end{array}
$$

since 199 is $2 \times 98 + 3$.

This computation explains itself. For the moment, we disregard the figures in the circles. If our guess for the dollars is correct, then the 4190 must represent 98 times the cents number. To get the cents number we divide this by 98. The trouble is, we get a fraction for this number, since there is a remainder; a discrepancy which for an integral result should be 0. Our assumption of 20 for the dollars number cannot then be correct. Let us trace the effect on the discrepancy, the remainder 74, of an increase by 1 in the assumed value for the dollars number. The figures in the circles show that the resulting effect on the remainder is an increase of 199. Now, when we consider merely the question of the quotient's being integral or not, multiples of the divisor, 98, do not affect the nature of the remainder. Clearly, since the dividend is to be increased by 199, and 199 is twice the divisor 98 plus 3, the remainder is affected simply by the 3. In other words, every increase by 1 in the assumed value for the dollars number means an increase of 3 in our discrepancy (the remainder). Similarly, a decrease of 1 in the assumed value implies a decrease by 3 in the remainder. We note that since 3 does not go into 74, we cannot hope to eliminate this remainder by decreasing our assumed dollars value. The only other alternative is to increase this value until the remainder grows to a multiple of the divisor. Now, the remainder differs from the divisor by 24. And 24 is 8×3. Hence,

187

if we increase our assumed value by 8 we should get an integral value for the cents number. But it appears that we get a whole series of such possible values. For example, we may go beyond the 8, and increase our assumed value by 98 more, or twice 98, etc. In other words, our correct values for the dollars figure would be any of the numbers 28, 126, 224, 322, etc. This is correct, so far as we have gone. But in this discussion we have not yet allowed for the requirement that the number of dollars must also serve as the number of cents on a cheque, and as such cannot be more than 99. Thus the only possibility for the dollars number is 28. The face value of the cheque is then $28.59.

Another problem

Suppose we consider an essentially similar problem:

A rancher stocked a new farm by spending $7885 for cows at $45 a head and bulls at $67 a head. How many of each did he buy?

As before, let us make a tentative assumption. Suppose he bought 100 cows. We have then the following computation:

Cost per cow	45
Assumed number of cows	100 $(+1)$
Cost of cows	4500 $(+45)$
Total cost	7885
Amount left for the bulls	3385 (-45)
Number of bulls.	50

$$67 \,) \, 3385 \;(-45)$$
$$\underline{335}$$
$$35 \;(-45) \text{ or } (67-45) \text{ or } (+22).$$

As before, the computation shows that every increase by 1 in our assumed number of cows involves a decrease by 45 in our dividend or a corresponding increase of 22 in the remainder. Correspondingly, if we decrease our assumed value by 1, the remainder is decreased by 22. We note that 67 differs by 1 from 3 times 22. We see that for every 3 by which we increase the number of cows the dividend is increased by 3×22, or 66. In other words, the remainder is thus reduced by 1. Now the remainder is 35. Hence we increase the assumed value of 100 by 35 3's, or 105, to get

205 cows. Further, we may eliminate the remainder by either of two other steps: First, we may merely add 67 to the previous value, 67 more to that, etc., and we may be assured that in each case we get an integral value for the number of bulls. Or, by the same token, we may subtract 67 from any acceptable number. What is equivalent to this is to increase the remainder till it is a multiple of the divisor. The remainder differs from the divisor by 32. Hence we subtract 32 3's from our assumed number of cows. Apparently, any one of the numbers 4, 71, 138, 205, etc., will suffice. Of course, they all differ by 67. Suppose we take any of these; say 4, the smallest. The computation now goes:

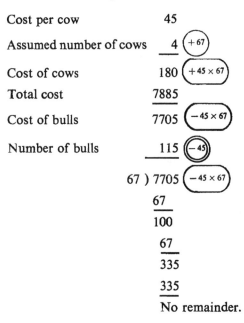

Cost per cow	45
Assumed number of cows	4 $(+67)$
Cost of cows	180 $(+45 \times 67)$
Total cost	7885
Cost of bulls	7705 (-45×67)
Number of bulls	115 (-45)

$$67 \,)\, 7705 \quad (-45 \times 67)$$
$$\underline{67}$$
$$100$$
$$\underline{67}$$
$$335$$
$$\underline{335}$$

No remainder.

Now, as we have seen, 4 cows is a possible answer. The remainder, our discrepancy, is reduced to nothing. Is that the only solution? Let us see: We have seen that the remainder is unaltered if we change the assumed number of cows by a multiple of 67. The recapitulation above shows that for every increase by 67 in the assumed number of cows there is, still without remainder, a reduction of 45×67 in the amount spent for the bulls. The number of bulls is $\frac{1}{67}$ of this. Hence the number of bulls is increased by 45 for every increase by 67 in the number of cows. How often can we increase the latter by 67? As often as we may subtract the 45 from 115! We see then that there are three, and only three, possible answers to our problem:

189

No. of Cows	No. of Bulls
4	115
71	70
138	25

Of course, the problem may be so worded, at least by implication, that only one of these answers would fit. Incidentally, where *no* possible answer would fit, this method will indicate that.

This method is general, and applicable to all problems of this type. For those who may be interested, the following analysis of an abstract case with comparatively large numbers should be sufficiently convincing.

A more general analysis

In all problems of this type using the +1 method, we always end up with a division where the divisor is fixed, there is also a remainder, and the quotient is increased (or decreased) by a certain number corresponding to this increase by 1 in the assumed value for one of the numbers involved in the problem. Our question is: Will the method illustrated above work for large numbers as well, where we cannot tell by inspection what multiple to use? Let us suppose for this purpose that we have to determine two numbers, say a number of A's and a number of B's. Suppose we assume a certain numbers of A's, say 100000, and that the number of B's then results from the division below:

$$
\begin{array}{r}
117524 \text{ No. of B's} \\
\hline
360529) \; 42370855962 \quad (+453916) \\
360529 \\
\hline
631795 \\
360529 \\
\hline
2712665 \\
2523703 \\
\hline
1889629 \\
1802645 \\
\hline
869846 \\
721058 \\
\hline
1487882 \\
1542116 \\
\hline
\text{Remainder} \quad 45766 \quad (+93387)
\end{array}
$$

We shall also suppose that, on repeating what we did in the last problem, a change of $+1$ in the assumed value for the A's results in a change of 453916 in the dividend, and hence in the remainder. But since we are dividing by 360529, and 453916 equals 360529 plus 93387, this is equivalent to increasing the remainder by 93387. We note again, that we either reduce the remainder to 0, or increase it by enough to make a multiple of the divisor, or reduce it beyond 0 by a multiple of the divisor. The point is, we seek only that modification which will make the quotient a whole number. We note in advance that, having determined a value for the A's which will make this division come out even, that result will also occur if we increase or diminish that number of A's by a multiple of the divisor. We look then for some such definite value.

We shall base our method on the familiar process of finding the greatest common divisor. The following computation is obviously correct, the significance of the numbers on the side being explained presently:

$$
\begin{aligned}
360529 &= 3 \times 93387 + & 80368 &- & 3 \\
93387 &= 1 \times 80368 + & 13019 &+ & 4 \\
80368 &= 6 \times 13019 + & 2254 &- & 27 \\
13019 &= 5 \times 2254 + & 1749 &+ & 139 \\
2254 &= 1 \times 1749 + & 505 &- & 166 \\
1749 &= 3 \times 505 + & 234 &+ & 637 \\
505 &= 2 \times 234 + & 37 &- & 1440 \\
234 &= 6 \times 37 + & 12 &+ & 9277 \\
37 &= 3 \times 12 + & 1 &- & 29271
\end{aligned}
$$

Now increasing the dividend by 360529 does not alter the remainder. Increasing it by 80368 is equivalent to increasing it by 360529 and decreasing it by 3 times 93387. Since each increase by 1 in the number of A's produces an increase of 93387 in the remainder, and a change by 360529 does not alter the remainder, an increase of 80368 in the dividend results from a decrease by 3 in the A's. Further, $13019 = 93387 - 80368$. Hence an increase of 13019 in the dividend is equivalent to an increase of 93387 followed by a decrease of 80368. The first results from an increase of 1 in the A's; the second, as we have seen, from an increase by 3. Hence an increase of 4 in the A's results in a net increase of 13019 in the dividend. Similarly, since $2254 = 80368 - 6 \times 13019$, an increase by 2254 is equivalent to an increase by 80368 followed by a decrease of 6 times 13019. The first results from a decrease by 3 in the A's; the second from a decrease of 6×4 in the A's, or a net decrease by 27. Similarly, to effect a net increase of 1749 in the dividend, or the remainder, involves an increase of 4 plus 5 times 27, or 139 in the A's. Again, an increase of 525 in the remainder results from a decrease of 27 plus 139, or a decrease of 166 in the A's.

Further, an increase of 234 in the remainder results from an increase of 139 plus 3 times 166, or 637 in the A's. Continuing, an increase of 37 in the remainder results from a decrease of 166 plus 2 times 637, or a decrease of 1440 in the A's. Also, an increase of 12 in the remainder results from an increase of 637 plus 6 times 1440, or an increase of 9277 in the A's Finally, an increase of 1 in the remainder results from a decrease of 1440 plus 5 times 9277, or a decrease of 29271 in the A's. Conversely, an increase of 29271 in the assumed number of A's yields a reduction by just 1 in the remainder.

The actual remainder we have is 45766. Hence we increase the assumed value for the A's by 45766 times 29271, or 1339616586. We may reduce this by any multiple of 360529. Dividing by the latter, the remainder is 251351. Hence the smallest possible value for the A's is 100000 plus 251351, or 351351. The corresponding number of the B's in each case is obtained from the division. Of course, the wording of the problem may restrict the admissible answers to only one of these values.

As a final illustration of the method discussed, we may consider the following problem:

> A speculating rancher bought horses (H) at $217 each, steers (S) at $142 a head and mules (M) at $173 each, spending $52394. He later sold them, respectively, at $263, $154, and $211 each, receiving $60038. How many of each did he buy?

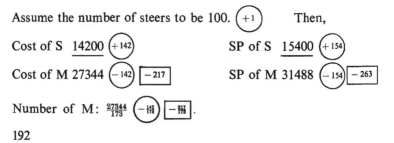

Assume the number of horses to be 50. $\boxed{+1}$ Then we proceed:

Cost of 1 H	217		SP of 1 H	263
Number of H	50 $\boxed{+1}$		Number of H	50 $\boxed{+1}$
Paid for H	10850 $\boxed{+217}$		Received for H 13150 $\boxed{+263}$	
Total paid	52394		Total received	60038
Cost of S and M 41544 $\boxed{-217}$			SP of S and M 46888 $\boxed{-263}$	

Now we have a subsidiary problem involving steers and mules:

Assume the number of steers to be 100. $\left(+1\right)$ Then,

Cost of S 14200 $\left(+142\right)$ SP of S 15400 $\left(+154\right)$

Cost of M 27344 $\left(-142\right)$ $\boxed{-217}$ SP of M 31488 $\left(-154\right)$ $\boxed{-263}$

Number of M: $\frac{27344}{173}$ $\left(-\textbf{₦}\right)$ $\boxed{-\textbf{₦}}$.

192

SP of M $\frac{27244}{173} \times 211 = \frac{5769584}{173} = 33350\frac{34}{173}$ $\left(-\frac{2999}{173}\right)$ 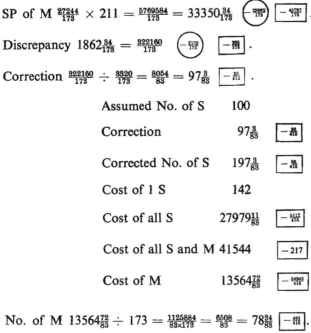 $\boxed{-\frac{4737}{173}}$.

Discrepancy $1862\frac{34}{173} = \frac{322160}{173}$ $\left(-\frac{1430}{173}\right)$ $\boxed{-\frac{788}{173}}$.

Correction $\frac{322160}{173} \div \frac{3320}{173} = \frac{8054}{83} = 97\frac{3}{83}$ $\boxed{-\frac{30}{415}}$.

Assumed No. of S   100

Correction $97\frac{3}{83}$ $\boxed{-\frac{30}{415}}$

Corrected No. of S $197\frac{3}{83}$ $\boxed{-\frac{30}{415}}$

Cost of 1 S   142

Cost of all S $27979\frac{11}{83}$ $\boxed{-\frac{5112}{415}}$

Cost of all S and M   41544 $\boxed{-217}$

Cost of M $13564\frac{72}{83}$ $\boxed{-\frac{64943}{415}}$

No. of M $13564\frac{72}{83} \div 173 = \frac{1125884}{83 \times 173} = \frac{6508}{83} = 78\frac{34}{83}$ $\boxed{-\frac{491}{415}}$.

Hence we have:

H 50 $\boxed{+1}$ S $197\frac{3}{83}$ $\boxed{-\frac{30}{415}}$ M $78\frac{34}{83}$ $\boxed{-1\frac{76}{415}}$

Obviously, the number of 1's we must add to 50 must be a multiple of 5, to reduce the denominator 415 to 83. So we have,

H 50 $\boxed{+5}$ S $197\frac{3}{83}$ $\boxed{-\frac{6}{83}}$ M $78\frac{34}{83}$ $\boxed{-\frac{76}{83}}$

So we ask, what multiple of 36 is 3 more than a multiple of 83? This is readily seen to be 7. Conveniently, this multiple of 76 also is 34 more than a multiple of 83. How this multiple can be found in every case is explained in the general discussion preceding this problem. Apparently, if we add 83 to this multiple, 7, we may get additional solutions. But then we would have to reduce the number of mules by more than we have done. So there is just one solution. This we get on applying the correction:

H		S		M	
	50		$197\frac{3}{83}$		$78\frac{34}{83}$
+	35	−	$3\frac{3}{83}$	−	$41\frac{34}{83}$
	85		194		37

193

Another type of whole number problem

We shall close this chapter with the analysis of another type of problem of which the following is a good example:

Six men visited a small deserted island in the South Seas. They gathered up in a huge pile all the cocoanuts they could find. During the night one of the men rose and decided to take his sixth of the cocoanuts. There was 1 over, which he ate. Later a second man rose and did the same with what he found, but there were 3 over, which he ate. Later still a third man did the same with the cocoanuts he found, but on taking a sixth there were 5 over, which he ate. A fourth man did the same, but found 1 over, which he ate. A fifth did the same, eating 3 that were left over. The last man did the same, eating the 5 that were left over after dividing by 6 what he found. In the morning no one said anything, and they divided the remaining cocoanuts between them, nothing being left over. How many cocoanuts were collected originally?

Of course, this is not a 'practical' problem. We shall solve it merely as an arithmetical exercise. Let us assume that there were 100000 cocoanuts in the whole pile. The first man found 1 more than a multiple of 6. On dividing the assumed 100000 by 6, there is a remainder of 4, not 1. Hence 100000 cannot be the number, but 3 less, or 3 more, or 6 more or less than that, etc., will be a satisfactory number, so far as we have gone. In other words, to make the first man's operation possible, we must have the following number of cocoanuts:
100003, or 100003 plus or minus any multiple of 6.
We shall denote this in short by writing

100003 plus or minus 6's.

Now one-sixth of 100003 is 16667 with 1 over. The last is the cocoanut the first man ate. He took so many cocoanuts (16667) plus or minus 1 for every modification of the whole number by 6. He left 5 times what he took. In other words, he left

83335 plus or minus 5's.

The second man took one-sixth of these, leaving 3 over to be eaten. Now one-sixth of 83335 leaves 1 over, not 3. So we have to alter this number to make the second man's operation also possible. But to make the first man's operation possible we must alter the last figure by a number of 5's. We may take two 5's less, for example. That would give 83325, which now leaves 3 over. But an alteration of every six 5's only will still leave 3 over on dividing by 6. In other words, 83325 will permit both the first two men to perform their actions, and the only other possible numbers that will also permit them are modifications of this number by six 5's, or 30. Hence the only numbers possible are

83325 plus or minus 30's.

The second man took 13887 plus or minus 5's, leaving 5 times as much, or

69435 plus or minus 25's.

This is what the third man found. The problem says that on dividing by 6 there were 5 left. But on dividing 69435 by 6 there are 3 left. Since each 25 that may be added to the number adds an additional 1 to the remainder, we suppose the number increased by two 25's, to 69485, which does leave 5 over on dividing by 6. But only by modifying this by six 25's at a time does this remain true. Hence the number of cocoanuts found by the third man must be 69485 plus or minus 150's. He took

11580 plus or minus 25's,

discarding 5 and leaving 5 times as much, or

57900 plus or minus 125's.

The fourth man found this, and that after eating 1 he could divide the remainder evenly by 6. Now on dividing 57900 by 6, there is no remainder. Also, if 125 be subtracted, the 57775 left would leave just 1 over. But then a modification of only every six 125's will permit the man to take his sixth. In other words, not any multiple of 125 may be added to or subtracted from 57775 to make all the actions possible so far, but only every 6 times 125, or 750. The fifth man must have found the following number of cocoanuts:

57775 plus or minus 750's.

He ate 1 and then took

9629 plus or minus 125's,

leaving

48145 plus or minus 625's.

The fifth man found a remainder of 3 on dividing by 6. But one-sixth of 48145 leaves 1. If we add two 625's to this number we get 49395, which does leave a remainder of 3. But only every sixth 625 will leave that possibility intact. In other words, the fifth man found a number of cocoanuts included in the following:

49395 plus or minus 3750's.

He ate 3 and then took

8232 plus or minus 625's,

leaving

41160 plus or minus 3125's.

The last man found a remainder of 5 on dividing by 6. But 41160 has no remainder. We add just one 3125, giving 44285, which does leave a remainder of 5. But only every six 3125's will ensure that. Hence the last man must have found a number of cocoanuts shown by the following numbers:

44285 plus or minus 18750's.

He ate 5, then took

7380 plus or minus 3125's,

leaving

36900 plus or minus 15625's.

In the morning each took one-sixth of this. Now 36900 is already divisible by 6, but 15625 is not. Hence we may modify the 36900 only by six 15625's, or by 93750, at a time. Hence the number of cocoanuts finally divided may have been 36900 (the least possible), or 130650, or 224400, or 318150, etc. In other words, the sixth man left a number of cocoanuts among the following:

36900 plus 93750's.

He had taken one-fifth of this, or

7380 plus 18750's.

Counting the 5 he had eaten, he had found

44285 plus 112500's.

This is what the fifth man had left. He had taken

8857 plus 22500's.

Counting the 3 he had eaten, he had found

53145 plus 135000's.

This is what the fourth man had left. He had taken

10629 plus 27000's.

Counting the 1 he ate, the fourth man had found

63775 plus 162000's.

This is what the third man had left. He had taken

12755 plus 32400's.

Counting the 5 he ate, the third man had found

76535 plus 194400's.

This is what the second man had left. He had taken

15307 plus 38880's.

Counting the 3 he ate, the second man had found

91845 plus 233280's.

This is what the first man had left. He had taken

18369 plus 46656's.

Counting the 1 he ate, the first man must have found

110215 plus 279936's.

Hence the number of cocoanuts gathered may have been 110215 or any multiple of 279936 more than that. The problem might have restricted the answer to the smallest of these by stating that there were, all told, less than a quarter of a million cocoanuts.

The explanation given here may seem tedious. However, in actually solving such a problem but little detailed writing need be employed. In fact, the entire procedure can be included in a simple tabular array. The procedure for this problem, too, shows how elementary arithmetic may be applied to solve an apparently complex problem.

Actually, this problem could have been solved in reverse, reducing the number of steps. In fact, the entire solution may be put into the following compact form:

Person	Left	Took	Found
All	0	Some each	6's
F	30's	5 + 6's	5 + 36's
E	185 + 180's	40 + 36's	225 + 216's
D	1305 + 1080's	262 + 216's	1567 + 1296's
C	5455 + 6480's	1096 + 1296's	6551 + 7776's
B	37655 + 38880's	7534 + 7776's	45189 + 46656's
A	91845 + 233280's	18370 + 46656's	110215 + 279936's

Exercises

1. Solve Ex. 26 of Ch. I.
2. Solve Ex. 27 of Ch. I.
3. Solve Ex. 28 of Ch. I.
4. Solve Ex. 29 of Ch. I.
5. Solve Ex. 30 of Ch. I.
6. Solve Ex. 31 of Ch. I.
7. Solve Ex. 32 of Ch. I.
8. Solve Ex. 33 of Ch. I.

9. Solve Ex. 41 of Ch. I.

10. Solve Ex. 34 of Ch. II.

11. Henry is twice as old as Betty was 5 years ago. Together their ages total 23 years. How old is Henry?

12. The sum of two numbers is 192. Four times their difference exceeds thrice the smaller by one-sixth of the difference. What are the numbers?

13. A certain fraction reduces to $\frac{2}{3}$. If, before reducing, we add 4 to both numerator and denominator, the fraction reduces to $\frac{7}{10}$. What is the fraction?

14. The ages of Father and Bill total 102 years. Father is now four times as old as Bill was when Father was twice as old as Bill is now. How old is Father?

15. Three times one number exceeds four times another by 12. Seven times the difference exceeds twice the sum by 6. What are the numbers?

16. Solve Ex. 46 of Ch. I.

17. Solve Ex. 47 of Ch. I.

18. A grocer wishes to mix coffee that cost him 35 cents a pound with another brand that cost him 61 cents a pound so as to get 100 pounds costing him $46.30. How many pounds of each brand should he use?

19. Do Ex. 51 of Ch. I.

20. Father is now half again as old as Fred will be 10 years hence. Father is also three times as old as Fred was when Father was twice as old as Fred was 6 years ago. How old is Father?

21. Two brothers, A and B, were in the habit of giving each other various sums as they needed them, in special reserve accounts. During an expected period of business activity they anticipated the following exchanges, as a result of which each would have the same amount of cash in reserve: A would give B $300; then B would give A 20% of his reserve; then A would give B 25% of his reserve; finally B would give A $1000. However, unexpected matters brought about the following series of exchanges: B gave A 5% of his reserve; then A gave B $510; then B gave A 20% of his reserve; then A had to give B $1120 to make both reserves equal. How much did each have in reserve initially?

22. Ambrose is 14 years younger than his brother Bernard will be at the time when Ambrose will be three times as old as Bernard was when Ambrose was half as old as both together will be 2 years hence. Further, Bernard is 2 years younger than half again as old as Ambrose was when both together were one half as old as Ambrose will be when Bernard is 1 year younger than Ambrose is now. How old is each of the brothers now?

23. A gentleman purchased an item for $1.32. He had not enough money with him, but tendered in payment a cheque he had received from one of his customers. He casually thrust the change into a side pocket.

On reaching home he found that the change was exactly three times the face value of the cheque, and noted that obviously the cashier of the store had inadvertently interchanged the figures of the dollars and cents. What was the face value of the cheque?

24. A lady purchased chairs at \$14 apiece and tablecloths at \$3 apiece. Finding she had spent nearly \$100, she decided to make the expenditure exactly \$100 by buying oranges at 6 for a quarter. All told, she thus bought 35 objects. How many of each did she buy?

25. A rancher bought a certain number of horses at \$119 each, cows at \$72 a head, and bulls at \$109 a head, spending \$12582 in all at the sale. Had he paid \$11 more for each horse, \$7 more for each cow, and \$6 less for each bull he would have spent \$13383 for the animals in the sale. How many of each kind did he buy?

26. A fruit dealer spent a certain sum in stocking apples, pears and bananas. He reflected that had he spent twice as much for apples and half as much for pears he would have had 5% of his whole outlay left for more bananas. On the other hand, had he spent twice as much for bananas and half as much for apples, he would have spent 27% less of all his money on pears. What part of his money went to each item of fruit?

27. In stocking a new ranch a cattleman spent his money on three items; chickens, sheep and cattle. On going over his figures he noted that if the percentage spent on cattle were increased by 5 and if he had bought one-fifth fewer sheep, he would have had left enough for twice as many chickens as he now had. On the other hand, if the percentage laid out for cattle were increased by 5, and he had bought two-fifths fewer sheep, he would have had enough left for half as many more chickens than he now had. What percentage of his outlay went for cattle, sheep and chickens?

28. Derive the three numbers used as the basis for the number trick in Ch. I.

29. Solve the cocoanut problem of the text on the assumption that the residues, in order, were 3, 2, 1, 3, 2, 1.

XI   MISCELLANEOUS PROBLEMS

In this final chapter we take up a few questions and exercises that are not readily classified under other headings or that require somewhat more technical treatment.

Probability

Many surprising results come from considering the quantitative aspects of chance. For example, the writer, who does not bet, has persuaded people to agree to wager even money when the chances were many thousands to one against them! Lest this be hard to believe, let us imagine posing a few questions to the uninitiated:

"If I tossed an ordinary coin, would you bet even money that it fell heads?" Most people would answer "Yes", they would. So we continue:

"If I tossed two coins at once would you bet even money that they fell divided, one head and one tail?" Here again most people would answer "Yes", they would. If not, they could soon be induced to give *some* odds, for or against, which we can proceed to magnify, as we do below:

"Well now, suppose I tossed four coins at once. Would you bet even money that they split even, two heads and two tails?" Here *some* people would say "Yes"; a few perhaps because they might believe the contrary was expected of them. Now in this case the odds are 5 to 3 against such an occurrence. *In the long run*, such a bettor is bound to lose. However, we do not wish to wait, particularly if we can achieve substantial certainty. So we continue:

"If I were to toss four coins simultaneously 2000 times in succession, would you bet even money, say $1000, that in at least 1000 of these tosses the coins would split even, two heads and two tails?" Once having committed himself to the previous answer, this is but a logical step. The answer is, inevitably, "Yes". If we really wished to bet, we could lower the figure 1000 to 975 or even 950, or, if the other is not to become too suspicious, to 900. Or else we might offer slight odds, say 10 to 9 against. However, in any case, the actual odds are many thousands to 1 against such a result.

A paradox

Apart from offering to try a large number of cases, the writer has found it difficult to make the following clear to people unfamiliar with the subject. We say:

"Suppose we select the thirteen Spades from an ordinary deck of cards, and you select seven of these cards at random. Would you wager even money that the seven you select would include the Ace?" Of course, the answer is generally "Yes". We continue:

"Suppose that instead of taking the thirteen Spades we took the thirteen Diamonds. Would you still bet even money that you could select the ace in seven tries?" Again the answer is, perhaps somewhat impatiently, "Yes", with a sneaking glance at us for signs of mental aberration. We continue:

"Suppose now that instead of the Spades, or the Diamonds, or either of the other suits, we take all four suits together, with four times as many cards and four times as many aces. Would you still bet even money that you would include an Ace in drawing seven cards?" Here some hesitate, but usually only because of a suspicion that they are being 'led on'. However, the answer is generally forthcoming; "Yes". Now what are the actual odds? In the first case, the odds are seven to six, or about 54 to 46. In the second case the odds are about 55 to 45 *against* choosing an ace! The first figure is quite obviously correct. In the second case, we proceed as follows: The chance of not including an ace in selecting a single card is $\frac{48}{52}$. Having selected a card not an ace, the chance that the next card, from the 51 left, is not an ace is $\frac{47}{51}$. Having selected two cards not including an ace, the chance of the third not being an ace is $\frac{46}{50}$; etc. Hence the chance that no ace be included among the seven cards selected is the product of all these seven probabilities, or

$$\frac{48}{52} \cdot \frac{47}{51} \cdot \frac{46}{50} \cdot \frac{45}{49} \cdot \frac{44}{48} \cdot \frac{43}{47} \cdot \frac{42}{46}$$

The chance of including an ace is then the difference between this fraction and 1. This turns out to be $\frac{3478}{7735}$. The odds are then 4257 to 3478 *against* one picking an ace. The underlying reason for that is that in the second form of the problem selecting more than one ace at a time counts for the same as selecting a single ace, and the chance of doing so is great enough to account for the difference in our percentage odds.

Sequential partitions

Ex. 42 of Ch. I is of a type that occurs frequently in the more difficult of the Magic Number Arrangements we discussed in Ch. VI. In such a case we are not concerned with the theoretical number of solutions possible but with some means for getting one actual solution. We have another problem; of arranging consecutive integers into m sequences of n numbers each, where every such sequence is in arithmetical progression with a prescribed number difference. The question arises: For what sets of common differences is a distribution possible? Further, not being given *any* common difference but requiring our *m* sets of equidistant numbers to have the same sum, poses quite an interesting, and often difficult, problem.

The last type of problem occurs also in a modified form, where the number of numbers is even, the integers paired as on a domino and all others with the same sum also paired. Here our requirements may apply to *either one* of a pair. This makes the analysis richer in possibilities but considerably more difficult, and allows for a wealth of ingenuity.

It is often convenient to associate these numbers with an equidistant set of points on a line, or pairs of points on a line, or a periodically reversing group of lines of points or point pairs. A simple problem under this heading is Ex. 94 of Ch. VI.

Logic

Fallacies and paradoxes in this category are legion, many of them facetious and highly amusing. In many puzzles in this field the question is merely one of devising a practicable method of exhaustive elimination. This is often accomplished with the aid of one or more tables. Though the author has composed a number of these, we shall not give much space to them in this book.

The "15-puzzle"

This represents a box with room for 16 square blocks, but holding only 15, numbered as shown. The problem is to move the blocks about within the box, one block at a time, so as to end up with all the blocks in the same position, except 14 and 15, which are interchanged.

1	2	3	4
5	6	7	8
9	10	11	12
13	14	15	

That is impossible. It may be shown by very elementary means that all possible arrays may be put into two categories of such a kind that it is always possible to change from any array in either category to any other in that category, but impossible to change from one in one category to any one in the other. The point is that the same type of elementary analysis will serve for other types of array with the same restriction of motion. We may state that this puzzle is comparatively old.

Cryptograms

Quantitative methods are often applied to the solution of cryptograms and ciphers. Relative probabilities and general frequencies are often used. The writer has compared a variety of numerical sequences in the solution of difficult Substitution Cryptograms.

The question of the "Worst" possible arrangement, as discussed in Ch. 1, first occurred to the author in attempting to formulate rules for procedure in the solution of difficult substitution cryptograms.

In this connection the writer may say that in the latter activity it soon became apparent that elaborate numerical analysis suffered from inbreeding; that all the work might be actually self-consistent and yet have nothing to do with the actual solution! In consequence such over-elaborate numerical analysis has been largely curtailed, if not quite abandoned.

A checkerboard problem

Suppose a square board be divided into 64 equal squares as shown and that the squares are in two shades, coloured alternately. The usual game of checkers is played on one of these coloured sets of 32 squares. Moves are

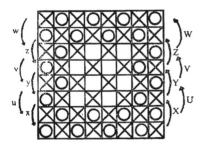

made only along diagonals from one square to another. In our problem only 'jumps' are allowed. Suppose two checkers p and q are on consecutive squares on a diagonal and that next to one of them, say q, there is a vacant square. Then p may jump over q to the vacant square beyond q, and q is then removed from the board. Ordinarily, the 'men' are of two colours. In our problem we make no distinction as to colour and none as to direction. We suppose the 24 men to be arranged initially as shown. The original problem then is this: Allowing only jumps of the type described, can 23 successive jumps be made, leaving only 1 checker on the board?

The fact that such a question is amenable to mathematical analysis is quite remarkable. Not less remarkable is the fact that the analysis necessary is so very elementary!

Let us number the rows from the bottom up and the columns from left to right. It is clear that every jump carries a checker 2 rows up or down the board and two columns to the right or the left. Now just before the final, the 23rd, jump is accomplished, after the 22nd jump, there are but two checkers left on the board. For the next jump to be possible these two checkers must be on consecutive squares on some diagonal. Hence they must be on adjacent rows and also in adjacent columns.

Now let X be the number of jumps upward from the first row, x the

203

number downward to the first row, U upward from the second row, etc., for all the symbols in the figure. The fact that one or more of these symbols might be 0 will not, as will be evident, affect our reasoning.

Now suppose that before our jumping frolic the rows contain a_1, a_2, a_3, a_4, a_5, a_6, a_7, a_8 checkers respectively and that at the end they contain b_1, b_2, b_3, b_4, b_5, b_6, b_7, b_8.

Consider the number of checkers in any row. That may be increased in only two ways, by having checkers jumping into that row from below, or from above. Again, it may be decreased in four ways; by jumping out of the row downward, by jumping out of it upward, by being jumped over from the row below, by being jumped over from the row above. Using the symbols we have introduced for these manoeuvres (see figure), we readily obtain these equations:

$$
\begin{aligned}
a_1 &\quad + x \quad - X \quad\quad\quad\quad\ = b_1 \\
a_2 &\quad + u \quad\quad - U - X - x = b_2 \\
a_3 &+ X + y \ - x - Y - U - u = b_3 \\
a_4 &+ U + v - u - V - Y - y = b_4 \\
a_5 &+ Y + z - y - Z - V - v = b_5 \\
a_6 &+ V + w - v - W - Z - z = b_6 \\
a_7 &+ Z \quad\quad - z \quad\ - W - w = b_7 \\
a_8 &+ W \quad\quad - w \quad\quad\quad\quad\ = b_8
\end{aligned}
$$

From the first and last of these,

$$X = a_1 - b_1 + x, \qquad w = a_8 - b_8 + W$$

Substituting, the remaining six equations become:

$$
\begin{aligned}
a_2 + u \ - U - 2x \ - a_1 + b_1 \quad\quad\ = b_2 \\
a_3 + y \ - Y - U \ - u \ + a_1 - b_1 = b_3 \\
a_4 + U + v - u \ - V - Y - y \ = b_4 \\
a_5 + Y + z - y \ - Z - V - v \ = b_5 \\
a_6 + V - v - Z \ - z \ + a_8 - b_8 = b_6 \\
a_7 + Z - z \ - 2W - a_8 + b_8 \quad\quad = b_7.
\end{aligned}
$$

From the first and last of these,

$$u = b_2 + U + 2x + a_1 - a_2 - b_1, \quad Z = b_7 + z + 2W + a_8 - a_7 - b_8.$$

Using these, the remaining four equations become:

$$
\begin{aligned}
a_3 + y \ - Y - 2U - 2x \ - b_2 \ + a_2 \quad\quad\quad\quad\quad = b_3 \\
a_4 + v \ - V - Y \ - y \ - 2x \ - b_2 - a_1 + a_2 + b_1 = b_4 \\
a_5 + Y - y - V \ - v \ - 2W - b_7 - a_8 + a_7 + b_8 = b_5 \\
a_6 + V - v - 2z - 2W - b_7 \ + a_7 \quad\quad\quad\quad\quad = b_6.
\end{aligned}
$$

Adding the first, second and fourth of these equations, then the second and third, then the first, third and fourth, we get

$$-2Y - 2U - 4x - 2z \ - 2W = \quad a_1 - 2a_2 - a_3 - a_4 - a_6 \ - a_7$$
$$- b_1 + 2b_2 + b_3 + b_4 + b_6 \ + b_7$$
$$-2V - 2y - 2x - 2W \quad\quad = \quad a_1 - a_2 \ - a_4 - a_5 - a_7 \ + a_8$$
$$- b_1 + b_2 \ + b_4 + b_5 + b_7 \ - b_8$$
$$-2U - 2x \ - 2v - 4W - 2z \ = \ - a_2 - a_3 \ - a_5 - a_6 - 2a_7 + a_8$$
$$+ b_2 + b_3 \ + b_5 + b_6 + 2b_7 - b_8.$$

Now, regardless of the values of the eight symbols involved, the three left members are even numbers. Hence the right members are even integers also. So each of the three expressions

$$A = (a_1 + a_3 + a_4 + a_6 + a_7) + (b_1 + b_3 + b_4 + b_6 + b_7)$$
$$B = (a_1 + a_2 + a_4 + a_5 + a_7 + a_8) + (b_1 + b_2 + b_4 + b_5 + b_7 + b_8)$$
$$C = (a_2 + a_3 + a_5 + a_6 + a_8) + (b_2 + b_3 + b_5 + b_6 + b_8)$$

all represent even numbers. Now, in our specific problem,

$$a_1 = 4, a_2 = 4, a_3 = 2, a_4 = 2, a_5 = 2, a_6 = 2, a_7 = 4, a_8 = 4.$$

Therefore each sum of b numbers must be even. Now, as we have seen, after 22 jumps, all but two b's must be 0 and the other two 1 each and *consecutive*. Suppose now $b_1 = b_2 = 1$ and $b_3 = b_4 = b_5 = b_6 = b_7 = b_8 = 0$. This violates the first and third of our equations. Hence the last two checkers cannot occupy the first and second rows, or, either by symmetry or by using our equations, the seventh or eighth rows. Of course, by the symmetry of our figure, the same applies to columns. Following the same procedure in the other few cases, we conclude that the solution of the problem as proposed is impossible. This problem is some 55 or 60 years old.

It will be seen that any two of the equations for A, B, C, determine the third. Again, on reviewing the analysis, it will be seen that these expressions must be even not only after the 22nd move but after *every* move. Also, after 22 moves, 11 men are removed from odd rows and 11 from even rows. Hence

$$X + Y + Z + x + y + z = U + V + W + u + v + w = 11.$$

Modified problems

Suppose the checker in the lower left hand corner is removed at the start and we are required to make the last jump into the vacated square. There are many solutions. We give one: Here a checker in the mth column and the nth row will be represented simply by mn, and a move will simply

connect the square of the checker with the square on which it lands. Then the following sequence of moves will suffice:
48-66, 75-57, 88-66, 68-46, 37-55, 15-37, 28-46, 13-35, 66-44, 44-26, 17-35, 35-57, 82-64, 71-53, 53-75, 84-66, 57-75, 86-64, 31-53, 64-42, 51-33, 33-11.

Now the requirement that we end up in Square 11 is curious. Suppose we had been required to finish on another square. What then? Let us see how it looks in the light of our equations. Here a_1 is odd, and the other a's even. We have consistence only when the last two checkers are either in the second and third rows or the fifth and sixth. Hence the final checker must be in the first, fourth or seventh rank. By symmetry of the setting, the same is true of the columns. Hence the only squares the last checker may be on are those numbered 11, 71, 44, 17, 77.

Suppose now that the 24 checkers are arranged to fill the first six rows. What then? It is clear that we need repeat no part of our analysis, since all the a's are still even, and that problem too is impossible. Suppose, then, one of these checkers is removed. Is it possible now? We have here 24 distinct problems. Curiously, if we apply our analysis by rows we get consistence in every case for certain pairs of rows. However, if we let our a's represent the numbers of checkers in the various columns we find consistence for some rows in 18 of the 24 cases. Inconsistence, indicating impossibility, is found when the checker is removed from any of the six squares in the third or sixth columns.

In the few cases of consistence the writer has tried there was no difficulty in finding solutions. In some way, then, the equations for A, B, C involve something basic that is inherent in the setting. Why that is so, the writer cannot say. One is almost forced to adopt a mystic attitude toward such matters. Possibly, in time, someone will evolve a way of analyzing or regarding a set of conditions which will make clear just what about them makes certain types of conclusions necessary or possible.

For an improved solution of the checkerboard problem, see SM for September-December 1954, pp. 206-8.

Chess and checkers

There are many incidental aspects of these games, particularly the second, which are capable of either mathematical formulation or analogy. Such points of view help in coordinating various positions and systematizing our mental pictures of them.

However, a mathematical analysis of either game is quite out of the question. The writer may say unequivocally that all those publications purporting to give a complete mathematical analysis of either game, or a general mathematical formulation for the best moves to make in any position, are unadulterated frauds.

Many have raised the question as to the relative merits of the two games. Neither game has been analyzed. Either offers scope for the fullest powers of any person. Choice is merely a matter of taste. Neither is intellectually superior, though, to the writer, checkers smacks more closely of the habits of thought of the mathematician than does chess, but that too not exclusively so.

A mathematical aptitude test

We close this chapter with a Mathematical Aptitude Test which the author prepared some years ago. It should be clear that this purports to be a test of aptitude, not of knowledge. Nevertheless, it would be of interest to see what the more experienced student of mathematics makes of it in, say, 20 or 30 minutes:

1. $5 + 3 = ?$
2. $10 - 3 = ?$
3. $16 + 41 = ?$
4. $73 + 29 = ?$
5. $81 - 37 = ?$
6. $16 + 106 - 73 + 19 = ?$
7. $102 - 71 + 65 - 11 = ?$
8. $7 \times 3 = ?$
9. $16 \times 7 = ?$
10. $19 \times 17 = ?$
11. $324 \div 18 = ?$
12. $1024 \div 32 = ?$
13. $\frac{1}{2} - \frac{1}{4} = ?$
14. $\frac{1}{2} \times \frac{1}{3} = ?$
15. $\frac{3}{4} \times \frac{2}{3} = ?$
16. $\frac{4}{7} \times \frac{63}{32} = ?$
17. $\frac{1}{2} + \frac{1}{3} = ?$
18. $\frac{1}{2} - \frac{1}{3} = ?$
19. $\frac{1}{2} \div \frac{1}{3} = ?$
20. $\frac{1}{3} \div \frac{1}{2} = ?$
21. $5\frac{1}{2} \div 11 = ?$
22. $5\frac{1}{3} \div 16 = ?$
23. $7\frac{1}{2} + 2\frac{2}{3} - 5 = ?$
24. $6\frac{1}{4} + 3\frac{1}{3} + 2\frac{1}{2} = ?$
25. Find the Highest Common Factor (i.e., the largest whole number that divides all) of 18, 2, 24, 36.

26. Find the H. C. F. of 63, 36, 75, 40.
27. Find the H. C. F. of 24, 36, 71, 40.
28. Find the H. C. F. of 18, 42, 30, 72.
29. Find the H. C. F. of 42, 28, 63, 84.
30. Find the Least Common Multiple (i.e., the smallest whole number that is divisible by each) of 2, 3, 4, 5, 6, 10.
31. Find the L. C. M. of 3, 4, 6, 7, 10, 15.
32. A man buys a horse for $100 and sells it for $122. What % profit does he realize?
33. A man buys a radio for $80 and sells it for $90. What % profit does he realize?
34. A man sells a picture for $80, losing 20%. What did the picture cost him?
35. A man sells a motorcycle for $160 at a loss of 25% How much was that loss?
36. 15 is one and one-quarter times what number?
37. 45 is one and one-quarter times more than what number?
38. What % is equivalent to $\frac{1}{4}$?
39. What % is equivalent to $\frac{1}{3}$?
40. What % is equivalent to $\frac{1}{6}$?
41. What % is equivalent to $\frac{1}{2}$?
42. What % is equivalent to $\frac{3}{4}$?
43. What % is equivalent to $\frac{3}{8}$?
44. What % is equivalent to $\frac{1}{15}$?
45. What % is equivalent to $\frac{1}{16}$?
46. What simple fraction is close to $\frac{100}{199}$?
47. What simple fraction is close to $\frac{200}{301}$?
48. What simple fraction is close to $\frac{52}{87}$?
49. What simple fraction is close to $\frac{50}{117}$?
50. What simple common fraction is closest to 37%?
51. What simple common fraction is about 42%?
52. What simple common fraction is about 12%?
53. What simple common fraction is about 17%?
54. What simple common fraction is about 31%?
55. At 44 cents a dozen, how many oranges can one get for $2.75?
56. At 22 cents a dozen, how many apples can one get for $2.75?
57. A man bought his boy a bicycle, a pen and a pencil. The pen cost three times as much as the pencil, and the bicycle seventeen times as much as the other two. At the same rate, how many pencils could the man have bought for the same money?
58. A cooper can finish 6 barrels in 2 days. How many workers like him can finish 210 barrels in 7 days?

59. If one man can pick 80 lbs. of cotton in one day, how long will it take 6 men to pick 2400 lbs.?
60. If 3 men can fill a wagon with potatoes in 30 minutes, how long will it take 2 men?
61. If it takes 8 men 2 days to walk from New York to Boston, how long will it take 12 men?
62. A freight train a mile long running at a mile a minute enters a tunnel a mile long. How long will it take for the freight train to go completely through the tunnel?
63. By just estimating, would you rather receive 50% a year on your investment after 10 years or 10% compound interest for the period?
64. If the earth were composed of grains of sand, would you expect the number of grains to consist of over 50 digits?
65. A says that each boy of a class of 20 has at least one marble, that no boy has more than 18, and that no two boys have the same number of marbles. B states forthwith that A must be mistaken. Is such a criticism justifiable?
66. What are all the different integral factors of 96?
67. What is the sum of all the different integral factors of 28, exclusive of 28 itself?
68. Dad to son: "Here is a little job for you, for which I will pay you at the regular union wage of 60 cents an hour. This board is 1 ft. square. I want it cut into 6 strips 2″ wide. I know you can cut off 1 strip in 10 minutes. So go to it." How much did the boy earn?
69. The distance from New York to Albany is 150 miles. An express leaves Albany for New York at noon travelling at 60 miles per hour. Also at noon a freight leaves New York for Albany travelling at 30 miles per hour. At what time will they pass each other?
70. . . We have here five dots. In how many distinct ways may
    .   we select three so as to form a triangle?
   . .
71. . . . We have here nine dots. In how many distinct ways may
   . . .   we select four so as to form a square?
   . . .
72. In Ex. 71, starting at any dot, and coming back to it, draw a continuous line of the shortest length that will pass through all the points.
73. A circle 2″ in diameter is replaced by one 3″ in diameter. By what proportion is the circumference increased: $1\frac{1}{8}$, $1\frac{1}{4}$, $1\frac{1}{2}$, $1\frac{3}{4}$ or 2?
74. By what proportion is the area increased: $1\frac{1}{2}$, 2, $2\frac{1}{4}$, $2\frac{1}{2}$ or $2\frac{3}{4}$?
75. A ball 4 inches in diameter is replaced by one 6 inches in diameter. By what proportion is the volume increased: 2, $2\frac{1}{2}$, 3, $3\frac{3}{8}$ or 4?

76. By what proportion is the surface increased:

$1\frac{1}{2}$, 2, $2\frac{1}{4}$, $2\frac{1}{2}$ or $2\frac{3}{4}$?

77. A circle of radius 10″ is replaced by one of radius 11″. What is the % increase in area:

10, 15, 18, 21, 25, 30 or 35?

78. A sphere of radius 10″ is replaced by one of 11″. What is the % increase in volume:

15, 20, 25, 29.4, 33.1, 36 or 40?

79.

```
        A
  C          B
  B          C

  A          A
     C   B
```

Draw three closed loops, one including only the A's, one only the B's, and one only the C's.

80. Some of the ancients calculated the circumference of a circle as exactly three times the diameter. Comment on that.

81. Is it easier to swim across a stream one mile wide and back to the starting point than to swim one mile up and back?

82. If you hold a disc at arm's length, what diameter must it have so as to just cover the face of the sun, looking with one eye?

83. A structure has a large circular room for the first storey and a hemispherical dome for the second. A contractor required 800 gallons of paint for the ceiling of the first storey. How many gallons of paint must he estimate for the domed ceiling:

1000, 1200, 1400, 1600, 1800 or 2000?

84. The ancient Egyptians calculated the area of the adjacent figure to be the product of half the base by the length of one side. Is that a correct procedure?

85. Four thin unequal rods are joined end to end to form a closed chain. Two adjoining rods are left on the table and the fourth hinge point elevated. Suppose we sight from the middle point of one rod to the middle point of the opposite (non-joining) rod and do the same for the other two rods. Can the lines of sight ever cross?

86. A gardener fenced in a new plot 24 feet by 48 feet. He planned for a strip of grass 1 yard wide within the fence. Exactly how many square yards of sod must he order?

87. A man stands on a spot X. He moves forward 1 step, then 2 steps to the right, then 5 steps to the rear, then 7 steps to the left, then forward 3 steps, then 2 steps to the right. Where is he then?

88. 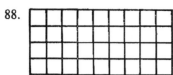 Show how to cut this figure into two pieces which can be fitted together to form a square.

89. The Yankees have won 3 out of 5 games against the Cardinals in a World's Series. If the teams are evenly matched in each game, what are the odds on the Yankees' winning? (Note: 4 games win the series.)

Exercises

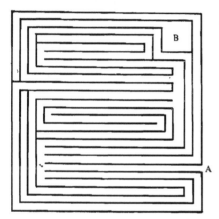

1. By inspection, see how quickly you can trace a way through the maze from A to B.

2. It is a remarkably windless day. Two aeroplanes race from New York to Chicago along the same route, one one mile up, the other two miles up. They manoeuvre till both are over the starting point and then race on. They average the same air speed. Is there any reason to expect one to arrive before the other?

3. Some mental exercise:
   1. 60 is $1\frac{1}{2}$ times more than what number?
   2. Caesar was assassinated in 44 B. C. What is the 2000th anniversary of that event?
   3. One student tells another he has dug up a relic in Rome dated 471 B. C. What might be the answer?
   4. Can the moon when half full ever rise at sundown?
   5. A middleman gets 60% off and gives 30% off. What % profit does he realize?
   6. How many letters are there in The Longest Word?

4. Some more mental exercise:
   1. Rome and New York are on the same parallel of latitude. An

211

aeroplane starts on the most direct route from New York to Rome. When leaving New York, does it travel due east?

2. How many is 6 dozen pairs less 5 gross?

3. What day of the week was it exactly 100 years ago?

5. Ibn Ben Hassim, Grand Mullah of a Near East sect, came to Baghdad three days before the start of the week-long annual religious festival. He made sure he was pure. If impure, he could be cleansed either by a week's fasting or by staying overnight in a house in which a pig was known to have been slaughtered. But if he did so when pure he thereby became unclean. After spending the night at the home of a friend, a neighbour told him of a rumour to the effect that a pig was once slaughtered in the friend's house. But he was not sure. Neither was the Mullah. Could you advise him?

6.

```
1   2   2   3   1
  3   2   3   2
3   1   2   3   1
  3   1   2   1
2   2   1   3   2
  3   1   1   3
```

Connect a number with two others by straight lines so that the sum of these is 6. Then similarly connect another such triad, etc., till all are connected. No lines are to cross or go through other numbers, and each number belongs to only one triad.

7. As in Ex. 6, connect triads that total 20 each:

```
10              5           5
         3           8
              1
      11                2
  6
   7           4   4
                        7
      6   12       13
   9    5       1       8
   3                   14
         7       9
   7         10       3
```

8. Can you follow directions?

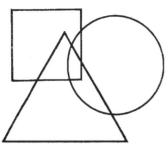

1. If the sun is a star, place a K in the space within the circle and square and without the triangle, and put a line through it; else put an E there facing backwards.

2. If choosing 7 socks blindly out of a bundle of socks with 6 designs will yield a pair, place an asterisk with a small circle round it in the circle without the square and the triangle; else write a small 'I' there with a dot over it.

3. At 12 o'clock a man moves the minute hand of a clock forward a whole number of spaces, then backwards a whole number of spaces, etc., for a number of moves, then back to 12 o'clock. If anything definite can be said about the total number of spaces moved place the number 3 within the three figures; else put the Roman number for 147 there.

4. If the sum of an even number of even numbers plus an odd number of odd numbers can never be the same as the sum of an even number of odd numbers plus an odd number of even numbers place a Q upside down in the triangle without the square and circle; else place a 7 there with a stroke through it.

5. If an eel is not a vertebrate place 4 small double E's in the space within the circle and triangle without the square; else put the Roman figure for one-third of a dozen there.

6. If the Earth's surface moves from west to east put a plus sign in the square without the circle and triangle; else place an interrogation mark there.

7. Given the six numbers 3, 8, 9, 7, 4, 5; if it is not false to deny that the average of the odd numbers is not less than that of the even numbers place an equals sign in the space common to the square and triangle without the circle; else place three dots with a loop round them there.

9. Suppose one watched an ordinary old-fashioned clock for 12 hours, starting at 1.17 p.m.
1. How many times would the clock strike once?
2. How many strokes would there be all told?
3. How many times would the hands be together?

10. . . . . How many sets of three of these dots will form triangles?
  . . . .
  . . . .

11. Suppose we have: a) A half ton of coal; b) 10 gallons of mercury; c) A cubic foot of gold. Which weighs most, which least?

12. . 160 . 175 . 201 . 136 . 121 . 103 .
  125 211 148   207 122 215

Twelve weights are hung from a beam at evenly spaced points, as indicated. If two pairs are interchanged, the beam will balance. Which?

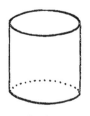

13. Sphere
Diameter 10 ft

Cylinder
Diameter 9 ft.
Height 9 ft.

Cone
Diameter 12 ft.
Height 12 ft.

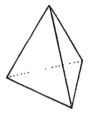

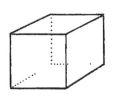

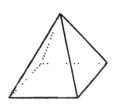

Regular Tetrahedron
Each side 15 ft.

Cube
Edge 8 ft.

Square pyramid
Base 11 ft. square.
Height 11 ft.

Arrange these six solids: a) By volume. b) By total surface. Do this first by just estimating, then, if you can, by computation.

14. These represent saucers each holding 6 beans. After the following five moves each still holds 6 beans. How?

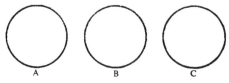

1. Leaving A intact, transfer 1 bean from one saucer to another.
2. Leaving B intact, transfer 2 beans from one saucer to another.
3. Leaving C intact, transfer 3 beans.
4. Leaving A intact, transfer 4 beans.
5. Leaving B intact, transfer 5 beans.

15. We wish to obtain in the fewest number of moves eight different multiples of 20 beans in the eight dishes represented. A move consists in taking some beans from one dish and placing all those taken in another dish. In how few moves can you do this?

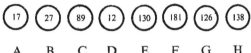

A   B   C   D   E   F   G   H

16. Four weights are sent to the ground from the top of the tower:

      A) Placed on pulley going down cable.

      B) Tossed upwards 2 seconds later at 16'/sec.

      C) Dropped $\frac{1}{2}$ second after releasing B.

      D) Thrown down with an initial velocity of 16'/sec. $\frac{1}{2}$ sec. after C is released.

      a) In what order do they land?

      b) What are their relative final velocities?

17. A drug store window across the street shows a large clear jar with a light behind it. Can we from our position tell whether or not the jar is full of water?

18. In the previous problem, suppose there is a light behind a red jar filled with liquid. Can we from our position determine whether it is a colourless glass with a red liquid or a red-tinted glass jar filled with water?

19. A line is cut into two segments one of which is used to form the perimeter of an equilateral triangle, the other the perimeter of a square.
a) What is the minimum sum of both areas?
b) What is the maximum?

20. Suppose the Earth an exact sphere 8000 miles in diameter, with a solid band round the equator and a belt stretched taut round that. Suppose now that a section of 6 feet were placed in the belt and a pole placed under the belt vertically till it was taut again.
a) What is the height of the pole?
b) What is the nearest point at which the belt touches the Earth?
   This will require an approximation by Newton's Method.

21. There are three containers. One, measuring 20 gallons, is empty. Two others, measuring 11 and 7 gallons respectively, are full of wine. There are no other containers or measures. How could the wine be divided equally between two?

22. As in Ex. 21, there are four containers, holding 4, 7, 10 and 15 gallons respectively. The largest is full. How could one divide it equally among three?

23. As in Ex. 21, there are six containers, holding respectively 4, 7, 11, 14, 17 and 25 gallons. The largest is full of wine. How could one divide that equally among five?

24. In rolling a pair of dice, if a 2, 3, 11 or 12 does not count, what are the odds in favour of the roller?

215

25. A Yarborough at Bridge is a hand of thirteen cards which contains nothing higher than a nine. In dealing a hand to four players at bridge, what is the probability that

a) a designated player will hold a Yarborough?

b) a Yarborough will be dealt?

We close with several problems which require some analysis:

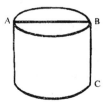

26. This represents a right circular cylinder. AB = a is a diameter of the upper base. BC = b is an element. What is the shortest distance from A to C along the surface of the cylinder?

27. Six dice are rolled simultaneously 200 times. What is the probability that in at least one pair of successive rolls there will appear first a total of 23, then 13?

28. A given line segment is cut into three pieces at random. What is the probability that the three smaller segments will form the altitudes of some triangle?

29. Prove by elementary methods that it is impossible to have four different integral squares in arithmetical progression.

Brooklyn, N.Y.   HARRY LANGMAN
January 14, 1951.

CPSIA information can be obtained
at www.ICGtesting.com
Printed in the USA
BVHW091947300121
599169BV00002B/312